Game Night Trivia: Part II

To Dylan

Never be afraid to chase your dreams. Love, Dad

Evan Salveson

Table of Contents

Introduction

Years ago, I would read books just to get facts and trivia. My mind was a sponge and it craved new information. I'd skim newspapers, encyclopedias, old school textbooks and anything else I could get my hands on. I loved to read biographies and history was easily my favorite subject. If I had a few dollars in my pocket I was buying baseball, basketball and football cards. I'd memorize jersey numbers, statistics and where every player went to college. But guess what? My grades weren't a reflection of how great my memory was or how much I loved to learn facts and trivia. I don't know how many times growing up I heard, "How come you can remember everyone's jersey number, but you can't remember to turn in your homework?"

Well many years later I know the answer to that question; I didn't have a passion for my homework. I certainly wish I would've tried harder in school, but this book and my other trivia books is just an ode to it's never too late in life to do what you love. I love writing and I love trivia. My hope is that a family will read this on a road trip or plane trip to a fun vacation site. Or a military member will read this to pass the time while he or she is on deployment.

Game Night Trivia: Part Two took a lot of hours to find what I hope are great trivia questions. I take great pride in putting out a solid product and I think (I know) that I've learned a lot in writing two previous trivia books. (*Game Night Trivia* and *The Trivia Matrix*) I hope you and those you share the trivia questions with will enjoy the book.

Don't be afraid to do or write about what you love. It could be something as simple as writing about trivia. Deep down we all have a passion. Mine is trivia.

Sincerely,

Evan Salveson

World History to Remember

"Those who do not learn history are doomed to repeat it."

1. What country's monarchy was overthrown during the 14 July Revolution? Iraq
2. What House of Plantagenet branch did House of York fight against in the War of the Roses? House of Lancaster
3. What high-ranking Nazi official was assassinated as the result of Operation Anthropoid? Reinhard Heydrich
4. To what island was Napoleon Bonaparte exiled to in 1814? Elba
5. What is the name of the revolution that overthrew China's Qing dynasty in 1911? Xinhai Revolution
6. Who was the wife to King Ferdinand II of Aragon? Isabella I of Castile
7. In what country did the 1937 Parsley Massacre occur? Dominican Republic
8. On what river was the ancient city of Babylon built? Euphrates
9. Who initiated the Salt March in 1930? Mahatma Gandhi
10. Who was Chairman of the Provisional Government of the Irish Free State? Michael Collins
11. Who succeeded Benito Mussolini as Prime Minister of Italy? Pietro Badoglio
12. Who was First Lady of Argentina at the time of her death in 1952? Eva Perón
13. How many laws comprise the Code of Hammurabi? 282 laws
14. What European king founded the Congo Free State? Leopold II of Belgium

15. In what country did the Boxer Rebellion take place? China
16. What faction did Alexander Bogdanov co-found? Bolsheviks
17. Who was the Archbishop of Canterbury that was murdered in 1170? Thomas Becket
18. Mustafa Atatürk was the first President of what country? Turkey
19. D. F. Malan began instituting apartheid as Prime Minister of what country? South Africa
20. Jochi was the eldest son of what ruler? Genghis Khan
21. Who was the first Tsar (Czar) of Russia? Ivan IV
22. During what war was the Battle of the Somme fought? World War I
23. Who led the coup against Milton Obote and became President of Uganda in 1971? Idi Amin
24. Airlifts of food and supplies began arriving to what European city on June 26, 1948? Berlin
25. In what Central American country did the Contras battle the Sandinistas? Nicaragua
26. In what year did Mount Vesuvius erupt and bury Pompeii? 79 A.D.
27. What ruler suffered his only defeat at Battle of the Catalaunian Plains? Attila the Hun
28. It is believed that Machu Picchu was built as an estate for what Inca emperor? Pachacuti
29. In what country did Mulai Ahmed er Raisuli and his bandits kidnap Ion Perdicaris and his step-son in 1904? Morocco
30. Who led the 26th of July Movement? Fidel Castro
31. Traudl Junge was a personal secretary to what dictator? Adolf Hitler
32. Adrian IV is the only Pope to have been born in what European country? England
33. King Mongkut was king of what current country during the 1800's? Thailand (formerly Siam)

34. In what city did the Tiananmen Square protests of 1989 occur? Beijing, China
35. Who was the last leader of the Soviet Union? Mikhail Gorbachev
36. The throne of the Holy Roman Empire was continually occupied by what royal house from 1438 to 1740? House of Habsburg (Also called House of Austria)
37. Who was the Prime Minister that Yigal Amir assassinated on November 4, 1995? Yitzhak Rabin
38. Darien colony was founded by the Kingdom of Scotland on the land of what current country in 1698? Panama
39. What was the capital of the Old Kingdom of Egypt? Memphis
40. Who lead the first expedition to reach the South Pole? Roald Amundsen
41. Who succeeded Winston Churchill as Prime Minister of the United Kingdom in 1945? Clement Attlee
42. Who was the last Aztec Emperor? Cuauhtémoc
43. What is the name of the dynasty that was overthrown during the 1979 Iranian Revolution? Pahlavi dynasty
44. Kingdom of Gorkha is the former name for what modern day Asian country? Nepal
45. What was the name of the world's first artificial nuclear reactor? Chicago Pile-1
46. What New7Wonders of the World location was once the capital of the Nabataeans? Petra
47. Who was elected the first female Chancellor of Germany? Angela Merkel
48. What is the name of the castle that the shogun of the Tokugawa shogunate of Japan once called home? Edo Castle
49. Who was the first black Archbishop of Cape Town, South Africa? Desmond Tutu

50. What is the name of the woman who purposely stepped in front of King George V's horse at the Epsom Derby on June 4, 1913? Emily Davison
51. Who did the Jordanian Armed Forces battle during Black September in 1970? Palestine Liberation Organization
52. Who was leader of the Partisans during World War II? Tito
53. What country did Henry Morgan become Lieutenant Governor of? Jamaica
54. In what city was Archduke Franz Ferdinand of Austria assassinated? Sarajevo
55. Anschluss was the name of the annexation of what country in Nazi Germany? Austria
56. What Spanish conquistador captured and killed Incan emperor Atahualpa? Francisco Pizarro
57. The United States' invasion of what small nation was codenamed Operation Urgent Fury? Grenada
58. Who developed the smallpox vaccine? Edward Jenner
59. Who commanded all Allied ground forces during Operation Overlord (Battle of Normandy)? Field Marshal Bernard Montgomery
60. Nicolae Ceaușescu was the last Communist leader of what country? Romania
61. Who founded Quebec City? Samuel de Champlain
62. How many inmates were imprisoned at the Bastille when it was stormed on July 14, 1789? Seven
63. Who was the first European to discover the sea route to India? Vasco da Gama
64. Treaty of Nerchinsk set the border between Russia and what other country? China
65. Van Diemen's Land was the original name Europeans used for what island? Tasmania
66. In what year was the Great Fire of London? 1666
67. Who was looking for the Seven Cities of Gold when he discovered the Grand Canyon? Coronado

68. What 20th century war is also known as the Fatherland Liberation War? Korean War
69. In what African country did the War in Darfur take place? Sudan
70. In what country was Leon Trotsky assassinated in 1940? Mexico
71. What was the first country to enact women's suffrage? New Zealand
72. Who ran the first marathon between Marathon and Athens, Greece? Pheidippides
73. In what country was the Maginot Line built? France
74. What famous Russian did Felix Yusupov help assassinate in 1916? Grigori Rasputin
75. In what country did the Carlist Wars occur during the 19th century? Spain
76. Who founded the Mughal Empire? Babur
77. In what country did the Blackshirts form in 1923? Italy
78. Who was the mother of Queen Elizabeth I? Anne Boleyn
79. What was the name of the Hungarian Countess who was tried and convicted of multiple murders in 1611? Elizabeth Bathory
80. Who captained the second successful circumnavigation of the world? Francis Drake
81. What two current countries were formed as a result of the Velvet Divorce? Czech Republic and Slovakia
82. What explorer claimed Canada for France? Jacques Cartier
83. In what English city did the Peterloo Massacre occur on August 16, 1819? Manchester
84. What treaty granted Mexico its independence from Spain? Treaty of Córdoba
85. In what country did the Rose Revolution occur in 2003? Georgia
86. Who won the Orteig Prize in 1927? Charles Lindbergh

87. In what present-day country did the Maji Maji Rebellion occur in the early 20th century? Tanzania
88. What monarch did Alexandra Feodorovna marry in 1894? Nicholas II of Russia
89. In what country did the 1916 Easter Rising (Easter Rebellion) occur? Ireland
90. Who is the Scandinavian that founded the first Norse settlement on Greenland? Erik the Red
91. Who was the fifth Great Khan of the Mongol Empire? Kublai Khan
92. On what island country was Ferdinand Magellan killed while attempting to circumnavigate the world? Philippines
93. What is the name of the British ocean liner did German U-boat SM *U-20* sink on May 7, 1915? RMS *Lusitania*
94. Francisco de Orellana was the first person to successfully navigate what river? Amazon
95. In what Pakistan city was Osama bin Laden found and killed? Abbottabad
96. What is the name of the huge explosion that occurred in Siberia on June 30, 1908? Tunguska Event
97. What city-state did Athens fight against in the Peloponnesian War? Sparta
98. What is the name of the British nurse who was tried for treason and executed in 1915? Edith Cavell
99. Who was the first Pope to visit North America? Pope Paul VI (1965)
100. What was the first Naval battle in which aircraft carriers engaged each other? Battle of the Coral Sea (WWII)
101. By what name is the Anti-Fascist Protection Rampart better known as? Berlin Wall
102. What European monarch died on September 14, 1982? Grace Kelly
103. What did the Nimrod Expedition explore? Antarctica

104. What piece of art did Vincenzo Peruggia steal on August 21, 1911? *Mona Lisa*
105. In what country was Dolly the cloned sheep born in 1996? Scotland
106. In what city and country was the capital of the League of Nations located? Geneva, Switzerland
107. During what naval battle was Admiral Horatio Nelson killed? Battle of Trafalgar
108. What is the name of the Roman general who committed suicide after losing the Battle of Actium? Mark Antony
109. What country did Egypt declare its independence from in 1922? United Kingdom
110. In what current country did the Boer Wars occur? South Africa
111. The death of what individual lead to the 2011 English riots? Mark Duggan
112. How many total Roman Catholic Popes served during the 20th Century? 9
113. Where did *Curiosity* land in 2012? Mars
114. Who is known as "The Nazi who said sorry"? Albert Speer
115. What is the name of the former Australian Prime Minister that went missing and was later presumed dead in 1967? Harold Holt
116. What German physicist was the originator of quantum theory? Max Planck
117. Who was Chief of State of Vichy France (Free State) during World War II? Philippe Pétain
118. Who was the only survivor of the car crash that killed Diana, Princess of Wales in 1997? Trevor Rees-Jones
119. Mary Mallon is known to have spread what infectious disease? Typhoid (Typhoid Mary)
120. What kind of object is a Fokker Eindecker? Fighter plane
121. Who is regarded as the inventor of modern paper? Cai Lun

122. Benjamin Guinness was the first Lord Mayor of what capital city? Dublin, Ireland
123. What World War II operation was nicknamed Dynamo? Evacuation of Dunkirk
124. Who overthrew Libya's King Idris I in 1969? Muammar Gaddafi
125. Cedric Popkin is the person believed to have shot and killed what World War I fighter? Manfred von Richthofen (Red Baron)

Science & Nature Up Close

Science is Everywhere

1. What is the rarest human blood type? AB negative
2. What constellation's name in Latin means "lizard"? Lacerta
3. Where would you go to find the world's highest atmospheric pressure? Siberia
4. After hydrogen, what is the second most abundant gas that forms the Sun? Helium
5. What kind of galaxy is the Milky Way? Spiral galaxy
6. A halophile organism needs a high concentration of what compound to survive? Salt
7. How many degrees are in a heptagon? 900 degrees
8. What are the first 7 digits of Pi? 3.141592
9. What type of pancreatic cells produce insulin? Beta cells
10. What is the most abundant blood protein found in humans? Albumin
11. One unit of horsepower is equal to approximately how many watts? 746 watts
12. What is the name for the study of materials at very low temperatures? Cryogenics
13. What planet in our solar system has the most known satellites? Saturn
14. In what part of the cell is DNA found? Nucleus
15. What is the only naturally occurring fissile isotope? Uranium-235
16. What ailment does someone have if they are diagnosed with urolithiasis? Kidney stones
17. Does lightning travel at the speed of light? No
18. What is the largest three-digit prime number? 997

19. What kind of device is a Pascaline? Calculator
20. What does pH stand for? Potential of hydrogen
21. Which planet has the moon Callisto? Jupiter
22. Aqua fortis is more commonly known as what acid? Nitric acid
23. What type of cloud produces rain? Nimbus
24. How many vertices does a cube have? 8
25. Pi times the radius squared solves for the area of what? Area of a circle
26. Which is a better conductor of electricity: gold, copper or silver? Silver
27. Dromedary is a type of what mammal? Camel
28. What was the first infectious disease to be eradicated? Smallpox
29. Which portion of the brain produces oxytocin? Hypothalamus
30. What is the lightest metal? Lithium
31. What type of compound can act as both an acid and a base? Amphoteric
32. Landspout and waterspout are types of what weather event? Tornados
33. How many protons are in one oxygen atom? 8
34. What does the acronym PVC stand for in PVC pipe? Polyvinyl chloride
35. What was the first spacecraft to land on the Moon? *Luna 2* (*Lunik 2*)
36. What is nomophobia the fear of? Fear of being out of cellular phone contact
37. How many different types of vitamins are in the human body? 13
38. A barn is a unit of what? Area
39. What "royal water" can dissolve both gold and platinum? Aqua regia
40. What is the world's largest flower? Rafflesia arnoldii
41. Which element has the chemical symbol P? Phosphorous

42. How many groups are on the Periodic Table of Elements? 18
43. In which layer of Earth's atmosphere is the ozone layer? Stratosphere
44. What is the nearest-known star to the Sun? Proxima Centauri
45. What is diaphoresis? Perspiration
46. How many total cubic feet is a standard cord of wood? 128 cubic feet
47. Poisoning from what metal causes Itai-itai disease? Cadmium
48. What is the pH of healthy spinal fluid? 7.4
49. How many flavors of quarks are there? 6
50. Hippology is the study of what mammal? Horses
51. Which planet's year is shorter than its day? Venus
52. What is the International Systems of Units (SI) unit used often in chemistry for amount of substance? Mole
53. What metallic element is copper mixed with to create bronze? Tin
54. What type of clouds are the highest in Earth's atmosphere? Noctilucent clouds
55. What kind of substance causes cancer? Carcinogen
56. What poison is used on South American poison darts? Batrachotoxin
57. What theorem states "A squared plus B squared equals C squared"? Pythagorean theorem
58. What element was formally called hydrargyrum? Mercury
59. Is crude oil an acid or is it a base? It's neither
60. What is the only letter not used on the Periodic Table? J
61. What mammal is known to live the longest? Bowhead whale
62. Where is the world's largest collection of corium found? Chernobyl
63. How many grams are in a decagram? 10
64. What is considered the basic unit of life? The cell
65. What protein is used to make gelatin? Collagen
66. How many degrees is each angle in an equilateral triangle? 60 degrees
67. What type of object is Allan Hills 84001? Meteorite

68. How many strands make up human DNA? Two
69. What is the SI unit for frequency? Hertz
70. What is the reciprocal of 2? 0.05
71. What is the more common name for a thrombocyte? Platelet
72. To the nearest ten-thousand, how many gallons of water would it take to fill an Olympic size swimming pool? 660,430 gallons
73. What does a flame of burning hydrogen in air produce? Water
74. What are the two types of bone marrow? Red marrow, Yellow marrow
75. What highly contagious infection would result in Koplik's spots? Measles
76. What is the world's fastest growing plant? Bamboo
77. What is oscitation? Yawning
78. What human body system does the hypothalamus belong to? Limbic system
79. What is low if you have hypotension? Blood pressure
80. If something is anhydrous, what substance is it missing? Water
81. What gives weight to a physical object on Earth? Gravity
82. What is produced when the water droplets in fog freeze to objects? Hard rime
83. What seismic zone has produced the top 3 all-time largest North American earthquakes? New Madrid seismic zone
84. What gas is responsible for causing the greenhouse effect? Carbon dioxide
85. What do you have if you have cerumen? Earwax
86. What is the human appendix connected to? Cecum
87. What is the heaviest known organism? Pando (A tree in Utah)
88. What is the name for the organ of a flower that produces pollen? Stamen
89. What kind of infection is pyelonephritis more commonly known as? Kidney infection

90. Anthracite and bituminous are both kinds of what rock? Coal
91. Tides are causes by the gravitational pull of the Moon and what other celestial object? Sun
92. What marine mammal has the largest dorsal fin? Killer whale (Orca)
93. Protium is the most common isotope of what element? Hydrogen
94. Radial keratotomy is a procedure performed on what human organ? Eye
95. What speed is needed to achieve escape velocity and enter Earth's orbit? 25,000 mph
96. What is the name for the unit for electrical charge? Coulomb
97. How many pounds are in a long ton? 2,240 pounds
98. During what era was the Jurassic Period? Mesozoic Era
99. What is the most common compound of chlorine? Sodium chloride (Salt)
100. What type of whale can grow a long tusk? Narwhal
101. What is the solid form of carbon dioxide known as? Dry ice
102. What type of virus is the cause for the common cold? Rhinovirus
103. How many teaspoons of water would it take to fill a gallon? 768 teaspoons
104. Equinoxes occur yearly during what two months? March and September
105. How many categories of hurricanes are there? 5
106. To the nearest ten-million, how many miles is Earth's complete rotation around the Sun? 584 million miles
107. What is the name for a solution in which the concentration of solutes is greater outside the cell than inside it? Hypertonic
108. Sodium and potassium belong to which group on the Periodic Table? Alkali metals
109. How many protons does an alpha particle contain? 2
110. How many spiral arms does the Milky Way have? 4

Geography

Here, There and Everywhere

1. After London, what is the United Kingdom's second most populated city? Birmingham, England
2. What body of water separates Asian Turkey from European Turkey? Bosphorus
3. After China, India and the United States of America, what is the world's fourth most populated country? Indonesia
4. What body of water separates Russia and Alaska? Bering Strait
5. What is the Arctic Ocean's largest island? Victoria Island (Canada)
6. In what city would you walk across the Pont Neuf? Paris, France
7. Alphabetically, what African capital city is last? Yaoundé, Cameroon
8. Inside what current country is the ancient city of Carthage? Tunisia
9. In what country would you find the intact remnants of Hadrian's Wall? England
10. What volcanic explosion is considered the loudest sound ever heard in modern history? Krakatoa
11. What is the world's tallest brick building? Chrysler Building
12. What sea does Croatia border? Adriatic Sea
13. Flodden Wall was built to help protect what European city? Edinburgh, Scotland
14. What Greek temple was built in dedication to the goddess Athena? Parthenon
15. How many rooms are in the White House? 132

16. What lake was formed due to the collapse of Mount Mazama? Crater Lake
17. Republic of Macedonia was created after the breakup of what country? Yugoslavia
18. What is Europe's longest mountain chain? Scandinavian Mountains
19. How many of the world's countries start with Q? One (Qatar)
20. What is the official language of Cambodia? Khmer
21. What is the most visited museum in the world? Forbidden City
22. What is the largest hydraulically filled dam in the United States? Fort Peck Dam
23. After Mount Kilimanjaro, what is the second tallest mountain in Africa? Mount Kenya
24. What is the tallest freestanding structure in North America? CN Tower (Toronto)
25. The Matterhorn sits between the border of Switzerland and what other country? Italy
26. In which ocean is Chukchi Sea located? Arctic Ocean
27. Where would you find the world's largest active geyser, Steamboat Geyser? Yellowstone National Park
28. What is the largest city located entirely on the European continent? Moscow
29. In what country would you find the ruins of Tikal? Guatemala
30. What gulf separates Yemen and Somalia? Gulf of Aden
31. What is the world's tallest structure? Burj Khalifa (Dubai)
32. What is the name of the Mexican volcano that began erupting in 1943? Paricutin
33. What river is 4,258 miles long? Nile
34. What is the world's steepest residential street? Baldwin Street (Dunedin, New Zealand)
35. What is the last volcano on the European mainland to erupt? Mount Vesuvius

36. What is the largest island in the Caribbean? Cuba
37. To the nearest 100,000 miles, how many square miles is the land area of the United States? 3,537,438 square miles
38. Which U.S. state only has 3 counties? Delaware
39. In what European city is *The Little Mermaid* statue? Copenhagen, Denmark
40. What is the largest island in the Southern Hemisphere? New Guinea
41. The Bechuanaland Protectorate became what country in 1966? Botswana
42. What World Heritage Site can be found in Wiltshire, England? Stonehenge
43. What is the center of the Northern Hemisphere? North Pole
44. What fountain sits in front of the Palazzo Poli? Trevi Fountain
45. What country is home to Ngorongoro Crater? Tanzania
46. What castle was used as the main film location for the television series *Downtown Abbey*? Highclere Castle
47. How many stories tall is the Empire State Building? 102
48. In what European country would you find Po Valley? Italy
49. What is the world's largest museum? Louvre
50. What historic landmark would you be visiting if you went to La Cuesta Encantada (The Enchanted Hill)? Hearst Castle
51. What is the highest peak in the Cascade Range? Mount Rainier
52. In which U.S. state would go to visit Carlsbad Caverns? New Mexico
53. What is the largest of the three waterfalls that form Niagara Falls? Horseshoe Falls
54. What country is home to the westernmost point in Europe? Portugal
55. What is the official language of Greenland? Greenlandic
56. What is the most densely populated South American country? Belize

57. What continent is home to Alice Springs? Australia
58. In what gulf is Bight of Bonny located? Gulf of Guinea
59. What European country is home to peace lines (walls) that were built to separate Catholics and Protestants? Northern Ireland
60. After the Dead Sea, what is the second-lowest lake in the world? Sea of Galilee
61. Along with Spain and France, what is the only other country to have both Mediterranean Sea and Atlantic Ocean coastlines? Morocco
62. What is the only landlocked country in Southeast Asia? Laos
63. What is the largest territory of the United States? Puerto Rico
64. What European city is home to the world's largest ancient castle? Prague (Prague Castle)
65. What is the largest city in the French Riviera? Nice, France
66. In what country are the Nazca Lines located? Peru
67. Puget Sound belongs to what sea? Salish Sea
68. In what U.S. National Park would you find Half Dome? Yosemite National Park
69. Kariba Dam shares its location with Zambia and what other African country? Zimbabwe
70. What is the smallest African country? Seychelles
71. How many miles long is the Panama Canal? 48 miles
72. In what country would you find remnants of the ancient city of Troy? Turkey
73. How many landlocked countries are there in North America? Zero
74. Natives of what African country are called "Cha-bos"? Chad
75. Hook Lighthouse is the oldest operating lighthouse in what country? Ireland
76. What is the southernmost latitude where the Sun can be directly overhead? Tropic of Capricorn
77. What is the world's longest river to flow entirely within one country? Yangtze (China)

78. What non-European country has the most Dutch speaking citizens? Suriname
79. What is Europe's most sparsely populated country? Iceland
80. What was the capital of West Germany? Bonn
81. What U.S. state capital has the highest elevation? Santa Fe, New Mexico
82. What is the world's driest non-polar desert? Atacama Desert in South America
83. What parallel separates Canada and Montana? 49th parallel
84. Gotland is an island that belongs to what country? Sweden
85. What is the most populated city in Florida? Jacksonville
86. What is the deepest point in Earth's seabed? Challenger Deep
87. What is the world's largest enclave landlocked country? Lesotho
88. What is the world's highest mountain outside of Asia? Aconcagua (Argentina)
89. Aside from the oceans, what is the world's largest biome? Taiga
90. What is Siberia's highest peak? Mount Belukha
91. The Euxine Sea is better known by what name? Black Sea
92. Which is the least populated of New York City's boroughs? Staten Island
93. What continent has the highest average elevation? Antarctica
94. Volcán Wolf is the highest point on what island group? Galapagos Islands
95. What is the world's northernmost metropolitan city? Helsinki, Finland
96. How many U.S. states were fully or partially created through the Louisiana Purchase? 15
97. What is the poorest country in Europe? Moldova
98. What is the highest summit of the Rocky Mountains? Mount Elbert
99. What capital city changed its name from Edo in 1868? Tokyo

100. What is the northernmost state in the continental United States? Minnesota
101. What is the only survivor of the Seven Wonders of the Ancient World? Great Pyramid of Giza
102. What is the highest capital city in Europe? Andorra la Vella
103. What U.S. rock formation was originally called Temple of Aeolus? Angels Landing
104. What is the elevation of Antarctica at the South Pole? 9,300 feet
105. What was the first 8,000 meter (26,200 feet) mountain to be summited? Annapurna I (Nepal)
106. What is the most densely populated island city in North America? Manhattan, NY
107. What world landmark is found in the city of Agra? Taj Mahal
108. Into what body of water does the Euphrates river drain? Persian Gulf
109. What is the name of the deepest limestone cave in the United States? Tears of the Turtle Cave
110. In what country is the rock fortress Sigiriya located? Sri Lanka
111. What continent has the most landlocked nations? Europe
112. What South American region encompasses the world's largest tropical wetland area? Pantanal
113. To the nearest 1 million, how many square miles is the world's total land area? 57,393,000 square miles
114. Which U.S. state is highest in mean elevation? Colorado
115. What are the only two double landlocked countries in the world? Bhutan and Uzbekistan
116. The largest portion of the Kalahari Desert is situated inside what African nation? Botswana
117. What is the deepest lake in North America? Great Slave Lake

118. After Cairo, what is the second largest city in the Arab world? Baghdad
119. In what city and state is the Thaddeus Kosciuszko National Memorial? Philadelphia, Pennsylvania
120. What river feeds Grand Canyon of the Yellowstone? Yellowstone river
121. Surtsey is the southernmost point of what country? Iceland
122. How many mountain peaks have an elevation higher than 28,000 feet? 3
123. Besides the Blue Nile, what is the other main tributary of the Nile? White Nile
124. What type of glacier is a Piedmont glacier? Valley
125. Bab-el-Mandeb (Gate of Tears) connects Gulf of Aden to what sea? Red Sea
126. What country's highest mountain is Snowdon? Wales
127. Where is the largest public bison herd in the U.S.? Yellowstone National Park
128. What is the largest landlocked country in South America? Paraguay
129. Argentina, Chile and what other country comprise the Southern Cone of South America? Uruguay
130. In what Canadian territory is the Klondike region? Yukon
131. Aotearoa is the Māori name for what country? New Zealand
132. Split is the second-largest city in what European country? Croatia
133. What is the southernmost state in New England? Connecticut
134. How many countries border both China and Russia? 14
135. Which Seven Wonders of the Ancient World was destroyed by the 1303 Crete earthquake? Lighthouse of Alexandria
136. In what U.S. state is Bad Rock Canyon located? Montana
137. What is the most populous metropolitan area in the world? Tokyo, Japan

138. What is both the highest peak in Mexico and the highest volcano in North America? Pico de Orizaba
139. What is the most densely populated U.S. state? New Jersey
140. In what Asian capital city is Chiang Kai-shek Memorial Hall? Taipei, Taiwan
141. Which is the southernmost Scandinavian country? Denmark
142. What is the official language of Ivory Coast? French
143. Which country is bigger in total area: Italy, Spain or Germany? Spain
144. What country is located closest to Antarctica? Argentina
145. In which ocean is the Ring of Fire? Pacific Ocean
146. What U.S. state is nicknamed The Diamond State? Delaware
147. Which Great Lake is Chicago located on? Lake Michigan
148. What U.S. state is home to Naval Base Kitsap? Washington
149. What is Maine's most populated city? Portland
150. Rabat is the capital of what country? Morocco

Sports Junkie

Take it to the house

1. Who is the oldest person to ever score an NFL touchdown (non-throwing)? Doug Flutie
2. How many total teams were in Major League Baseball when the Chicago Cubs won the 1908 World Series? 16
3. What does GSH stand for on the uniforms of the Chicago Bears? George Stanley Halas
4. What North American soccer club did Pelé play during the 1970's? New York Cosmos
5. What was the original name of the National Football League before changing its name in 1922? American Professional Football Association
6. Actor Mark Harmon's dad Tom Harmon won the Heisman Trophy while playing for what university? University of Michigan
7. What is the best finish for the United States men's team in the FIFA World Cup? 3rd Place (1930 World Cup)
8. Who was the only fighter to knockout Floyd Patterson in consecutive bouts? Sonny Liston
9. What is the last event of a decathlon? 1,500-meter run
10. Who was the first player to sign with Major League Soccer? Tab Ramos
11. Who was the first San Francisco 49er to win NFL MVP? John Brodie
12. From what country does MMA fighter Conor McGregor hail from? Ireland
13. What country was originally selected to host the 1986 FIFA World Cup? Colombia
14. Who was the first winner of the Hickok Belt? Phil Rizzuto

15. Who is the all-time leader in passing yards for the USFL? Bobby Hebert
16. What did Hans-Gunnar Liljenwall become the first athlete to fail? Olympic drug test
17. What heavyweight boxing champion was nicknamed Boston Strong Boy? John L. Sullivan
18. Who was the first father-son duo to hit back-to-back home runs in an MLB game? Ken Griffey Jr. and Sr.
19. Who was the first player to record a triple-double in the NBA All-Star Game? Michael Jordan
20. Who was the last NFL player to play a game without a helmet? Dick Plasman
21. Who is the only MLB player to win a Gold Glove Award as both an outfielder and as an infielder? Darin Erstad
22. Who is the only male wild card entrant to win a Wimbledon title? Goran Ivanišević
23. What is the name of the athletic mascot for the University of Texas at Austin? Bevo
24. Who was manager of the Birmingham Barons the season Michael Jordan played for them? Terry Francona
25. What NFL team did Vince Lombardi take over as head coach and general manager for after leaving the Green Bay Packers? Washington Redskins
26. Who was the first female Naismith College Player of the Year? Anne Donovan
27. How many minutes is a golfer allowed to search for a lost ball? 5-minutes
28. What was the original name of Wrigley Field? Weeghman Park
29. What does BMX (biking) stand for? Bicycle moto x
30. As of 2017, who is the last undisputed heaving boxing champion? Lennox Lewis
31. What racing event always takes place the first Saturday in May? Kentucky Derby

32. What two countries played in the first cricket test match? Australia and England
33. What was the first African nation to qualify for the FIFA World Cup? Egypt
34. Who is the only special teams player to win NFL MVP? Mark Moseley (1982)
35. Who was the first tennis player to win the Golden Slam by winning all four Grand Slam singles titles and the Olympic gold medal in the same calendar year? Steffi Graf
36. What was the first NFL team to win five Super Bowls? San Francisco 49ers
37. Who was the first American to manage an English Premier League club? Bob Bradley
38. Who batted behind Joe DiMaggio when DiMaggio made his Major League Baseball debut? Lou Gehrig
39. Who is the only head coach to win three Super Bowls with three different starting quarterbacks? Joe Gibbs
40. Who was the first New York Knick to lead the NBA in scoring? Bernard King (1984-85)
41. What jersey number did Michael Jordan wear when he un-retired and rejoined the Chicago Bulls? 45
42. Where did Dwayne "The Rock" Johnson play college football? University of Miami
43. Who was the first MLB pitcher to hit two home runs in the same game he threw a no-hitter? Rick Wise
44. What Brazilian soccer club tragically lost 19 players in a 2016 plane crash? Chapecoense
45. The international hall of fame for what sport is in Canastota, New York? Boxing
46. Who was the first player to score four goals in his NHL debut? Auston Matthews
47. How many teams from the American Basketball Association joined the NBA following the ABA-NBA merger in 1976? 4

48. Who is the English Premier League's all-time leading goal scorer? Alan Shearer
49. Who was the first tennis player to earn one-million dollars in a single season? Bjorn Bjorg
50. Who was the first MLB player to record 4,000 regular season hits? Ty Cobb
51. When was the last time England won the FIFA World Cup? 1966
52. Who is the last NBA player to average 30 points and 15 rebounds per game for an entire season? Bob McAdoo
53. What professional soccer club signed Tim Howard in 2003? Manchester United
54. Who was the first head coach for the Jacksonville Jaguars? Tom Coughlin
55. Who holds the Major League Baseball record for most games played without appearing in a World Series? Rafael Palmeiro
56. What NBA team was Dick Vitale head coach of in the late 1970's? Detroit Pistons
57. Who was the first non-quarterback or non-running back to win NFL MVP? Alan Page
58. Who was the first person inducted into the Basketball Hall of Fame as both a player and coach? John Wooden
59. Who was the first U.S. President to appear on the cover of *Sports Illustrated*? John F. Kennedy
60. Who was the first soccer player to win four European Golden Shoe awards? Cristiano Ronaldo
61. What team won the last USFL Championship? Baltimore Stars
62. What current NBA team was once the Buffalo Braves? Los Angeles Clippers
63. Who is the youngest winner of a Grand Slam singles title? Michael Chang
64. Ryan Giggs and Paul Scholes played their entire careers for which English Premier League club? Manchester United

65. How many furlongs is the Kentucky Derby? 10
66. What Pro Football Hall of Famer was born in Port Angeles, WA? John Elway
67. Who was the first North American to win a professional sports championship as a player, coach, and executive? Pat Riley
68. What NFL quarterback was suspended due to "Deflate Gate"? Tom Brady
69. Who holds the NBA record for most career assists? John Stockton
70. What was the name of the original home field for the Pittsburgh Steelers? Forbes Field
71. Who gave Evander Holyfield his first professional loss? Riddick Bowe
72. What U.S. professional sports team has been in the same city and with the same name for the longest period? Philadelphia Phillies
73. In what sport might you see a bicycle kick? Soccer
74. Having played their home games in the Cycledrome, what was the last team to win an NFL Championship that is no longer in the league? Providence Steam Roller
75. To the nearest foot, how tall is the Green Monster at Fenway Park? 37'2"
76. Against what hitter did Nolan Ryan record his 4,000th career strikeout? Danny Heep
77. What U.S. city was originally awarded the 1976 Winter Olympics? Denver, Colorado
78. How many times did Babe Ruth win the World Series as a member of the New York Yankees? 4
79. What NFL team originally signed Kurt Warner as an undrafted free agent? Green Bay Packers
80. What British Open winner's autobiography is titled, *All My Exes Wear Rolexes*? John Daly

81. What was the first European country to win the FIFA World Cup? Italy (1934)
82. What NBA player earned the nickname, "Vinsanity"? Vince Carter
83. Who was the first MLB player to earn $10 million dollars in a single season? Albert Belle
84. Who managed Leicester City to the 2016-17 English Premier League title? Claudio Ranieri
85. Who was the first overall pick in the 1975 NBA Draft, and the first guard to score 70 points in an NBA game? David Thompson
86. Who was the first coach to win hockey's "Triple Gold Club" (Stanley Cup, Olympic Games gold medal and World Championship gold medal)? Mike Babcock
87. Who headbutted Marco Materazzi at the 2006 FIFA World Cup? Zinedine Zidane
88. In what sport would you find umbrella and mushroom positional set ups? Water polo
89. Wilt Chamberlin and what other player were the first NBA players to average 30 points scoring in a single season in 1959-60? Jack Twyman
90. Ajax and PSV Eindhoven are professional soccer clubs that play in what country's league? Netherlands
91. What team holds the NBA regular season record for most wins? Golden State Warriors
92. How many times did Mickey Mantle hit 50 or more home runs in a season? 2
93. What was the first dome sports stadium in the United States? Astrodome
94. Who was the oldest member of the 1992 USA Olympic "Dream Team"? Larry Bird
95. What soccer confederation does Mexico, Canada and the USA belong to? CONCACAF

96. How many laps would you need to complete on a 400 meter track to complete an entire marathon? 105.5
97. Who was the first coach to win both a college football championship and a Super Bowl? Jimmy Johnson
98. Who was the first player from the University of Louisville to win the Heisman Trophy? Lamar Jackson
99. Who was the first NFL quarterback to throw for over 500 yards in a game? Norm Van Brocklin
100. Who was the first three-time winner of the Naismith College Player of the Year award? Bill Walton
101. What was the first sports franchise with a valuation of $3 billion by *Forbes*? Manchester United Football Club
102. Who was the first woman to buy a Major League Baseball club? Marge Schott (Cincinnati Reds)
103. Who is the older brother of Eli and Peyton Manning? Cooper Manning
104. What former Edmonton Oiler scored the final goal in WHA (World Hockey Association) history? Dave Semenko
105. Who recorded the first 58 in an official PGA tournament round? Jim Furyk
106. Who did Buster Douglas lose to in his first fight after defeating Mike Tyson? Evander Holyfield
107. Who was the first Japanese born player to hit a home run in the World Series? Hideki Matsui
108. Who succeeded Alex Ferguson as manager of Manchester United? David Moyes
109. Who was the first left-handed quarterback elected to the Pro Football Hall of Fame? Steve Young
110. Who was skipper of the first defender to be defeated in the 132-year history of the America's Cup? Dennis Conner in 1983
111. What is the official name of the trophy given to each season's World Series Champion? The Commissioner's Trophy

112. What city hosted the first Olympic games in which females competed? Paris (1900)
113. Who was the first Major League Baseball player to hit 30 home runs and steal 30 bases in the same season? Ken Williams (1922)
114. Who did Bill Belichick succeed as head coach of the New England Patriots? Pete Carroll
115. Who was the first Heisman Trophy winner to play in a Super Bowl? Mike Garrett
116. Who was the first NASCAR driver to appear on the cover of *Sports Illustrated*? Curtis Turner
117. Who was the last MLB player to have played in the Negro Leagues? Hank Aaron
118. Who won the only U.S. gold medal at the 1968 Winter Olympics? Peggy Fleming
119. What is the Japanese term for a professional sumo wrestler? Rikishi
120. Who was the first NHL player to reach 500 career goals? Maurice Richard
121. What is the name of the Japanese professional wrestler that Muhammad Ali signed up to fight in 1976? Antonio Inoki
122. Who is the oldest NHL player to ever record a hat trick? Jaromir Jagr
123. Who was the first player to win an NBA title, NCAA title and multiple Olympic gold medals? Michael Jordan
124. Who was the first wide receiver in NFL history to record 100-yard games with four different quarterbacks in the same season? DeAndre Hopkins
125. Who is the all-time leading scorer for the former Seattle Supersonics franchise? Gary Payton
126. What university hosts the Little 500 bicycle race? Indiana University

127. Who was the first 3-time winner of the Baseball Writers' Association of America's Most Valuable Player award? Jimmie Foxx
128. What club did Wayne Rooney rejoin in 2017? Everton Football Club
129. Who was the first Brazilian Formula One world champion? Emerson Fittipaldi
130. In NFL rules, how many yards is the penalty for roughing the passer? 15 yards
131. Who was the first player to go directly from the Negro Leagues to Major League Baseball? Larry Doby
132. What American-born player was drafted #1 overall in the 2016 NHL Draft? Auston Matthews
133. Who was the first woman to score over 7,000 points in a heptathlon event? Jackie Joyner-Kersee
134. Who was the first boxer to win a divisional world championship five times? Sugar Ray Robinson
135. Who was the Sherpa for Edmund Hillary when he reached the summit of Mount Everest? Tenzing Norgay
136. Who is the youngest player to represent the United States men's national soccer team in a World Cup qualifier? Christian Pulisic
137. What was the last country to host the Olympics that is no longer a country? Yugoslavia
138. Who was the first Daytona 500 winner not born in the United States? Mario Andretti
139. Who was the first American to win Wimbledon? Bill Tilden (1920)
140. Who is the youngest person ever elected to the Baseball Hall of Fame? Sandy Koufax
141. Who was the first head coach of the New York Titans (Later becoming the New York Jets)? Sammy Baugh
142. Who holds the record as the youngest undisputed heavyweight boxing champion? Floyd Patterson

143. Where did Brett Favre play his college football? Southern Miss
144. Who is the oldest jockey to win the Kentucky Derby? Bill Shoemaker
145. What country has competed in the most Summer Olympics without winning a single gold medal? Philippines
146. Who is the only person elected to both the Naismith Memorial Basketball Hall of Fame and the Baseball Hall of Fame? Cumberland Posey
147. Who was the first player in NBA history to register 25 points, 20 assists and 10 rebounds in a game? Oscar Robertson
148. Who was the first American swimmer to qualify for five Olympic games? Michael Phelps
149. What is the national sport of New Zealand? Rugby union
150. Who was the first person of color to a win a Grand Slam tennis title? Althea Gibson (1956 French Open)
151. Who is the only defenseman to win the NHL scoring title? Bobby Orr
152. Who was the first female to win the Bob Jones Award (golf)? Babe Didrikson Zaharias
153. What professional soccer club plays its home matches at Santiago Bernabéu Stadium? Real Madrid
154. Babe Ruth played his final season in Major League Baseball with what team? Boston Braves
155. At what site was Super Bowl I played? Los Angeles Memorial Coliseum
156. What is the most common wood used to make Major League Baseball bats? Ash
157. Who was the Brooklyn Dodger executive that signed Jackie Robinson? Branch Rickey
158. Who did Gregg Popovich succeed as head coach of the San Antonio Spurs? Bob Hill

159. What Major League Baseball team had the first all-black outfield? San Francisco Giants (Willie Mays, Hank Thompson, Monte Irvin)
160. How many minutes long is half-time in the English Premier League? 15 minutes
161. The winner of what race receives the Borg-Warner Trophy? Indianapolis 500
162. What team won the first World Series that was held in 1903? Boston Americans (Red Sox)
163. Who was head coach of the Vegas Golden Knights for their inaugural NHL season? Gerard Gallant
164. Who was the first athlete to win a gold medal in the same individual event in four consecutive Olympics? Al Oerter (Discus)
165. Who was the first Kansas City Royal to win All-Star Game MVP? Bo Jackson
166. Who was the first draft pick in NBA history? Chuck Share (1950)
167. Who is the only person to ever win NBA MVP, NBA Finals MVP, and the NBA Sixth Man Award? Bill Walton
168. Who is the all-time hits leader for the Boston Red Sox? Carl Yastrzemski
169. Who was the first American to play in the English Premier League? John Harkes
170. Who is the only person to have his name on the Stanley Cup as both a player and owner? Mario Lemieux
171. Who was the first manager to win the World Series in both the National and American Leagues? Sparky Anderson
172. Dennis Martinez was the first Major League Baseball player from what country? Nicaragua
173. In the NFL, how many players must be lined up on the line of scrimmage? 7
174. The Grand Départ is the official start of what race? Tour de France

175. Who is the youngest Major League Baseball player to reach 4,000 career hits? Ty Cobb
176. Who is the only person enshrined in the both the Pro Football Hall of Fame and the Baseball Hall of Fame? Cal Hubbard
177. Who was the first NBA player to make 400 3-pointers in a single season? Stephen Curry
178. Doc Blanchard was the first junior to win what award? Heisman Trophy
179. Who did the Chicago Cubs make the first African American coach in Major League Baseball? Buck O'Neil
180. Who was the commissioner of Major League Baseball that handed Shoeless Joe Jackson a lifetime ban? Kenesaw Mountain Landis
181. What former NBA head coach holds the record for being ejected the most times? Don Nelson
182. What Vietnam War veteran won four Super Bowl rings with the Pittsburgh Steelers? Rocky Bleier
183. Who was the first and only offensive lineman to be named NFL Most Valuable Player? Mel Hein
184. What professional sport tournament awards the Wanamaker Trophy? PGA Championship
185. Who is the youngest driver to win the pole for the Daytona 500? Chase Elliott
186. Who was the first fighter to go 10 rounds with Mike Tyson? Quick Tillis
187. Who is the only driver to win the Daytona 500, Indianapolis 500, 24 Hours of Le Mans and the 24 Hours of Daytona? A.J. Foyt
188. Who was the first person to win a College Football National Championship, the Heisman Trophy, NFL MVP and the Super Bowl? Marcus Allen
189. Who was the youngest member of the 1992 USA Olympic "Dream Team"? Christian Laettner

190. What event in 1999 holds the record as the most-attended women's sports event in history? 1999 FIFA World Cup final
191. The Kangaroo Hoppet is an annual event in what winter sport? Cross-country skiing
192. Where did Billie Jean King and Bobby Riggs play their "The Battle of the Sexes" match? Astrodome
193. What was the final score of the USA vs USSR hockey game at the 1980 Olympic games? 4-3
194. Who fought Sugar Ray Robinson in a legendary fight nicknamed the Saint Valentine's Day Massacre? Jack LaMotta
195. What #1 overall pick in the 1973 NFL draft played the character Sloth in *The Goonies*? John Matuszak
196. Who did the PAC-12 football conference name as offensive player of the century? John Elway
197. What is the national sport of Russia? Bandy
198. Who is the all-time leading scorer in American Basketball Association (ABA) history? Louie Dampier
199. What former Boston Bruin was the first black NHL player? Willie O'Ree
200. What was the first thoroughbred to win the "Grand Slam" of American Thoroughbred racing? American Pharoah
201. What former Brazilian player is the first and only player to have appear in three World Cup finals? Cafu
202. What golfer won the first FedEx Cup in 2007? Tiger Woods
203. What legendary former wrestler coached University of Iowa to 15 NCAA team titles? Dan Gable
204. Who was the first player drafted straight out of high school to play in the NBA in the same year? Daryl Dawkins
205. Who is the NBA all-time leader in blocked shots? Hakeem Olajuwon
206. What Kansas City Chief running back died in 1983 attempting to save three children from drowning? Joe Delaney

207. Who was the first golfer to shoot a round of 62 in major championship history? Branden Grace
208. Who holds the record for the most rushing touchdowns with 6 in an NFL game? Ernie Nevers
209. What is the name of the German boxer that Joe Louis fought in 1936 and again 1938? Max Schmeling
210. Against what team did Babe Ruth hit his first MLB home run? New York Yankees
211. What is the maximum allowed weight in ounces of a regulation golf ball? 1.620 ounces
212. What nation's rugby team is called the Springboks? South Africa
213. What NHL team was once nicknamed the "Broad Street Bullies"? Philadelphia Flyers
214. Who was drafted #2 behind Peyton Manning in the 1998 NFL Draft? Ryan Leaf
215. What retired professional surfer is nicknamed "Mr. Smoothy"? Rob Machado
216. Who is the youngest player ever to be ranked World No. 1 by the Women's Tennis Association? Martina Hingis
217. Who was the first designated hitter for the Boston Red Sox on April 6, 1973? Orlando Cepeda
218. Who was the first and still only posthumous Formula One world champion? Jochen Rindt
219. Who was the first sitting U.S. President to attend a NASCAR race? Ronald Reagan
220. Who won the first MLS Golden Boot in 2005? Taylor Twellman
221. What former player won a World Series with the Milwaukee Braves and three NBA Championships with the Boston Celtics? Gene Conley
222. What is the name of the racehorse that was stolen from Ballymany Stud in Ireland on February 8, 1983? Shergar

223. Who was the first golfer to be awarded the Presidential Medal of Freedom? Arnold Palmer
224. Who won the Wimbledon Ladies' Singles Championship when she was just 15 in 1887? Lottie Dod
225. What Cleveland Indians player died after being hit in the head by a Carl Mays pitch? Ray Chapman

Music Maniac

I secretly wanted to be a radio DJ

1. What is the name of the English musical group Neil Tennant and Chris Lowe formed in 1981? Pet Shop Boys
2. What was the most requested song on FM radio stations during the 1970's? "Stairway to Heaven"
3. Besides George Michael, who was the other member of the duo Wham!? Andrew Ridgeley
4. Who was the original bass player for The Beatles? Stuart Sutcliffe
5. What band's live reunion album is titled *Hell Freezes Over*? The Eagles
6. What Rock & Roll Hall of Famer died on January 1, 1953 in Oak Hill, West Virginia? Hank Williams
7. Before the death of their lead singer Ian Curtis, the musical group New Order went by what name? Joy Division
8. Who played the harmonica on Elton John's song, "I Guess That's Why They Call It the Blues"? Stevie Wonder
9. What singer launched the Femme Fatale Tour in 2011? Britney Spears
10. What is the title of Kanye West's debut album? *The College Dropout*
11. Onika Tanya Maraj is better known as what recording artist? Nicki Minaj
12. What is the only Van Halen song to reach #1 on the *Billboard* Hot 100? "Jump"
13. The Stone Roses originated in what England city? Manchester

14. What hip hop group was Nelly with before starting his solo career? St. Lunatics
15. What multi-platinum selling band's former name was Hybrid Theory? Linkin Park
16. What hip hop group that originated in Oakland, CA was Tupac Shakur a member of before his solo career? Digital Underground
17. Who was the first female solo artist inducted into the Country Music Hall of Fame? Patsy Cline
18. Who is 'The Starchild' member of the rock band KISS? Paul Stanley
19. In what city did the band Journey formed? San Francisco
20. What album by Coldplay was the world's top selling album in 2008? *Viva la Vida or Death and All His Friends*
21. What pop group did Ricky Martin start his career with? Menudo
22. Who sang the theme song "Good Ol' Boys" for the TV show *The Dukes of Hazzard*? Waylon Jennings
23. On what Queen album was "Bohemian Rhapsody" first released? *A Night at the Opera*
24. Who had the first *Billboard* Hot 100 #1 single without having a recording contract? Lisa Loeb
25. Greg Graffin is the lead singer of what punk rock band? Bad Religion
26. Who was the first artist in history to have seven albums that all achieved diamond status in the United States? Garth Brooks
27. What is the name of Eminem's 1996 debut album? *Infinite*
28. *The Piper at the Gates of Dawn* was the debut studio album for what English rock band? Pink Floyd
29. What rapper is the son of jazz musician Olu Dara? Nas
30. What heavy metal guitarist died in a plane crash on March 19, 1982 in Leesburg, FL? Randy Rhoads

31. "Reflection" by Christina Aguilera was the theme song for what Disney movie? *Mulan*
32. Who did 50 Cent lose the 2004 Grammy Award for Best New Artist to? Evanescence
33. Where was Jimi Hendrix's final concert performance? 1970 Isle of Fehmarn 'Love and Peace Festival'
34. Marc Bolan, Bill Legend, Mickey Finn and Steve Currie formed what English rock band? T. Rex
35. What fellow country singer did Faith Hill marry in 1996? Tim McGraw
36. *The Great Rock 'n' Roll Swindle* is a film based on what Rock and Roll Hall of Fame punk rock band? Sex Pistols
37. Who is called "The Godfather of Shock Rock"? Alice Cooper
38. Who were the four singers that comprised the "Million Dollar Quartet" 1956 impromptu jam session at Sun Record Studios? Johnny Cash, Elvis Presley, Carl Perkins, Jerry Lee Lewis
39. What 1989 film featured Peter Gabriel's song "In Your Eyes"? *Say Anything*
40. From what country does the musical group Of Monsters and Men originate? Iceland
41. What 1994 Soundgarden studio album has the songs "Spoonman" and "Fell on Black Days"? *Superunknown*
42. Who replaced Ozzy Osbourne in Black Sabbath? Ronnie James Dio
43. What band did Randy Meisner leave in 1977? The Eagles
44. What was the last song Bob Marley performed live onstage? "Get Up, Stand Up"
45. What rapper was born Artis Leon Ivey Jr.? Coolio
46. What heavy metal band was Dave Mustaine fired from before starting Megadeth? Metallica
47. What singer was on the cover of both *Time* and *Newsweek* in 1975? Bruce Springsteen

48. How old was John Lennon when he was murdered in 1980? 40
49. What rock band released the 1978 single "Sweet Talkin' Woman"? Electric Light Orchestra (ELO)
50. After which band member's death did Led Zeppelin decide to disband in 1980? John Bonham
51. What was the name of the group that Simon Le Bon and two other members of Duran Duran formed in 1985? Arcadia
52. What was the first hip hop song to reach the Top 5 on the *Billboard* Hot 100? "Walk This Way"
53. In what year did The Beatles first appear on *The Ed Sullivan Show*? 1964
54. Who was MTV's first world premiere video? "Thriller"
55. What hip hop group did Lil Wayne join in 1996? Hot Boys
56. Where did The Beatles perform their final paid concert? Candlestick Park, San Francisco
57. What artist released *Pieces of You* in 1995? Jewel
58. What musician was Michael J. Fox imitating when he performed "Johnny B. Good" in *Back to the Future*? Chuck Berry
59. What #1 single for charity did Bob Geldof and Midge Ure co-write in 1984? "Do They Know It's Christmas?"
60. What was the first video to win the Grammy Award for Best Music Video? "Hungry Like the Wolf"
61. What was the first country song to be certified diamond? "Cruise" by Florida Georgia Line
62. *Out of Step* was the only full-length studio album by what punk band? Minor Threat
63. Who was the first artist to top the *Billboard* Hot 100 based solely on airplay? Aaliyah for "Try Again"
64. What was the first *Billboard* #1 single for Prince? "When Doves Cry"
65. What late singer did The Dream Academy dedicate their song "Life in a Northern Town" to? Nick Drake

66. Who did Russell Simmons co-found Def Jam Recordings with in 1983? Rick Rubin
67. What rapper founded Ruthless Records in 1986? Eazy-E
68. *Sketches for My Sweetheart the Drunk* is a collection of songs that was released posthumously for what singer after he drowned in 1997? Jeff Buckley
69. Who was the first female artist to simultaneously have two albums in the Top 5 of the *Billboard* 200? Adele
70. What indie rock band consists of husband and wife Win Butler and Régine Chassagne? Arcade Fire
71. What Rock and Roll Hall of Fame band was founded in Athens, GA? R.E.M.
72. Who recorded the jazz album, *Birth of the Co*ol? Miles Davis
73. Who was the drummer for Nirvana? Dave Grohl
74. Which member of The Beatles is wearing denim on the cover of *Abbey Road*? George Harrison
75. What artist did the soundtrack for the movie *Into the Wild*? Eddie Vedder
76. What rock singer created the Cabo Wabo Tequila brand? Sammy Haggar
77. What was the first rap LP to be #1 on the *Billboard* album chart? *Licensed to Ill* (Beastie Boys)
78. Who did Paul McCartney collaborate with for the #1 song, "Ebony and Ivory"? Stevie Wonder
79. Who holds the record for the most number-one hits on *Billboard*'s Hot Country Songs chart? George Strait
80. Who shot and killed Marvin Gay? His father Marvin Gay Sr.
81. Who was the first Canadian to have double diamond album sales? Alanis Morissette
82. Hillel Slovak was the original guitarist for what Rock and Roll Hall of Fame band? Red Hot Chili Peppers
83. What American folk singer died in a plane crash on September 20, 1973 in Natchitoches, LA? Jim Croce

84. Neil Diamond's "Sweet Caroline" is played by what Major League Baseball team during every home game? Boston Red Sox
85. What movie had the top selling movie soundtrack of the 1990's? *The Bodyguard*
86. What jazz saxophonist was nicknamed Yardbird? Charlie Parker
87. What singer had the alter ego of Ziggy Stardust? David Bowie
88. What band opened 1969's Altamont Free Concert? Santana
89. Who was the first all-girl group to have a #1 single with the song, "Will You Still Love Me Tomorrow"? The Shirelles
90. What band's debut album is titled *Pretty Hate Machine*? Nine Inch Nails
91. What female singer's song was sampled into Eminem's single, "Stan"? Dido
92. Who performed "The Star Spangled Banner" at the original Woodstock? Jimi Hendrix
93. What was Elvis Presley's first released single? "That's All Right"
94. What former member of The Beach Boys died from drowning in 1983? Dennis Wilson
95. What soul musician released the soundtrack for the movie *Superfly*? Curtis Mayfield
96. What Rock and Roll Hall of Fame group did Ron "Pigpen" McKernan co-found? Grateful Dead
97. What was the worldwide top selling album of 1977? *Rumors*
98. What singer released her debut album *Katy Hudson* in 2001? Katy Perry
99. What Rock and Roll Hall of Fame band formed in Birmingham, England in 1968? Black Sabbath
100. Who did Michael Jackson co-write "We Are the World" with? Lionel Richie

101. What U.S. state named John Denver its poet laureate in 1974? Colorado
102. What band did Dave Grohl form after the death of Kurt Cobain caused Nirvana to disband? Foo Fighters
103. According to *Guinness World Records*, who is the best-selling female recording artist of all-time? Madonna
104. What is the name of the musical duo consisting of Alex Pall and Andrew Taggart? The Chainsmokers
105. Who wrote “Islands in the Stream” which was a duet by Kenny Rogers and Dolly Parton? The Bee Gees
106. What girl group was originally called Girl’s Tyme? Destiny’s Child
107. Who was the first female artist to achieve a UK number-one with a self-written song? Kate Bush
108. What Elvis Presley song did UB40 remake for the soundtrack to the movie *Sliver*? “Can’t Help Falling in Love”
109. What girl group did Camila Cabello leave in 2016? Fifth Harmony
110. What was Phil Collins’ debut solo single? “In the Air Tonight”
111. Which Tom Petty album featured the single “Free Fallin”? *Full Moon Fever*
112. Who did Joey McIntyre replace in New Kids on the Block? Mark Wahlberg
113. What is the name of Def Leppard’s drummer who lost his left arm in a 1985 car crash? Rick Allen
114. What album holds the record for the most consecutive weeks on the *Billboard* 200? *Dark Side of the Moon*
115. In what year did The Beatles breakup? 1970

General Trivia Time

An eclectic mix of everything

1. Who was the first woman placed on the FBI's Ten Most Wanted Fugitives list? Ruth Eisemann-Schier
2. What is the name for a word which reads the same backward as it does forward? Palindrome
3. What was the first U.S. state to register automobiles? New York
4. In what country would you find the Camargue region? France
5. What newspaper did both Bob Woodward and Carl Bernstein write for during the Watergate Scandal? *Washington Post*
6. Who was Leif Erikson's father? Erik the Red
7. Who did Ralph Fiennes depict in the film *Schindler's List*? Amon Goth
8. Who was the first person to reach 100 million Twitter followers? Katy Perry
9. What is the name for a solar day on Mars? Sol
10. What American frontiersman's life was the basis for *The Revenant*? Hugh Glass
11. In what European city is Palatine Hill located? Rome
12. The Committee for the Re-Election of the President (CREEP) was created for what former U.S. President? Richard Nixon
13. Who played Mr. Potter in *It's a Wonderful Life*? Lionel Barrymore
14. How many continuous main rings does Saturn have? 9
15. In the *Star Wars* movies, what kind of crystal powers a lightsaber? Kyber crystals
16. What was the first mail-order catalog in the United States? Tiffany's Blue Book

17. Who was the last Emperor of China? Puyi
18. Approximately how many miles are in one light-year? 5.88 trillion miles
19. Who was the last NFL player to wear 00 on his jersey? Ken Burrough
20. Who was the last surviving member of the Rat Pack? Joey Bishop
21. Who was the first winner of *American Idol*? Kelly Clarkson
22. Derecho is a type of what? Wind
23. Who was the first professional wrestler on the cover of *Sports Illustrated*? Hulk Hogan
24. What was the first novel to be blessed by a Pope? *Ben-Hur: A Tale of the Christ*
25. What was the first musical group to have six consecutive studio albums debut #1 on the *Billboard* 200? Dave Matthews Band
26. Who was the first republican U.S. President? Abraham Lincoln
27. What is the largest of the 88 recognized constellations? Hydra
28. What fort was originally called New Helvetia? Sutter's Fort
29. Who delivered the "We Shall Fight on the Beaches" speech on June 4, 1940? Winston Churchill
30. What Boston gang did Whitey Bulger belong to before going on the run? Winter Hill
31. The lights on the Las Vegas Strip were first dimmed as a show of respect after the death of what entertainer? Elvis Presley
32. What writer holds the record for the most combined Tony Award and Academy Award nominations? Neil Simon
33. What is the world's largest bay? Bay of Bengal
34. What was former First Lady Jackie Kennedy's maiden name? Bouvier

35. What film tells the story of Jamie "Jim" Graham? *Empire of the Sun*
36. What beverage did Charles Alderton develop during the 1880's? Dr. Pepper
37. On what continent is Queen Maud Land located? Antarctica
38. What was the longest conventional war of the 20th century? Iraq-Iran War
39. What is the world's largest capacity sports venue? Indianapolis Motor Speedway
40. What country's national legislature is the Knesset? Israel
41. What is the largest United State Native American tribe in terms of population? Navajo
42. What TV show holds the record as the longest-running American scripted primetime television series? *The Simpsons*
43. What does SSBN stand for in USS *Alabama* (SSBN-731)? Submersible Ship Ballistic Missile Nuclear
44. What was Africa's first national park? Virunga National Park
45. What is added to a hot pan when doing a Flambé? Alcohol
46. The substantia nigra is located in what human organ? Brain
47. On what island chain would you find Timanfaya National Park? Canary Islands
48. Who was the first English, Prince of Wales? Edward II
49. In *Bambi*, who is Bambi's future mate? Faline
50. Who did Mileva Marić marry in 1903? Albert Einstein
51. What is the largest city in New England? Boston
52. What type of insect would do a waggle dance? Honey bee
53. What is the name of the U.S. Army medic whose story was the basis for *Hacksaw Ridge*? Desmond Doss
54. What type of berry is predominately used to give gin its flavor? Juniper berries
55. What is the name of the revolution that led to independence for Latvia, Estonia and Lithuania? Singing Revolution
56. What is the name of the Middle White boar in *Animal Farm*? Old Major

57. In what French city is the Bastille located? Grenoble
58. What was the former official newspaper of the Communist Party of the Soviet Union? *Pravda*
59. What sea is sometimes called Erythraean Sea? Red Sea
60. What is the national fruit of both India and the Philippines? Mango
61. What is the name of Esmerelda's goat in *The Hunchback of Notre Dame*? Djali
62. Who was the host of *Howdy Doody*? Buffalo Bob Smith
63. What type of bird is a kakapo? Parrot
64. What are the brightest electromagnetic events that occur in the universe? Gamma-ray bursts
65. What is the name of the Chilean President who committed suicide on September 11, 1973? Salvador Allende
66. What politician that reported seeing a UFO in Leary, Georgia in 1969? Jimmy Carter
67. Who played Leon Carp in *Roseanne*? Martin Mull
68. What country was formally known as Siam? Thailand
69. What was Elaine's last name on *Seinfeld*? Benes
70. A hobbit is also known by what name? Halfling
71. What commander conquered more territory than anyone else in world history? Subutai
72. What kind of fiber is rayon? Cellulose fiber
73. Who discovered the Java Man remains? Eugene Dubois
74. Who was the second wife of Julius Caesar? Pompeia
75. What is the Hubble sequence used to classify? Galaxies
76. What is the world's longest barrier island? Padre Island
77. The Willow ptarmigan is the state bird of what U.S. state? Alaska
78. What was the name of Benito Mussolini's mistress who was executed with him? Clara Petacci
79. What sweetener that is used in sugar-free gum is also toxic to dogs? Xylitol

80. How many colored stickers are on a standard Rubik's Cube? 54
81. In what country was the revolutionary society Katipunan founded? Philippines
82. What river flows through London, England? River Thames
83. Who did Laura Ingalls marry? Almanzo Wilder
84. What did the White Rose resistance group oppose? Nazi Regime
85. In what William Shakespeare play is St. Crispin's Day speech told? *Henry V*
86. In what month does a Full Snow Moon occur for North America to see? February
87. How many provinces does Canada have? 10
88. What television actor played for MLS club Los Angeles Galaxy in 1996? Andrew Shue
89. What kind of milk is traditionally used to make Cendol? Coconut milk
90. Who was the only American that Adolf Hitler mentioned in *Mein Kampf*? Henry Ford
91. Who designed the Statue of Liberty? Frédéric Auguste Bartholdi
92. Who was married to Martin Luther King, Jr.? Coretta Scott King
93. What was the name of the boxer that Mr. T played in *Rocky III*? Clubber Lang
94. How many grams of sugar are in a 12-ounce can of regular Pepsi? 41 grams
95. What plant is the primary source for producing morphine? Opium poppy
96. Under what U.S. President was NASA founded? Dwight D. Eisenhower
97. What is the largest of Japan's islands? Honshu
98. What is the name of the character that Robert De Niro played in *Taxi Driver*? Travis Bickle

99. What kind of weapon is a falchion? Sword
100. What Nobel Prize winning author died on July 2, 1961? Ernest Hemingway
101. What was the name of the cargo ship that was hijacked in 2009 and later became inspiration for the movie *Captain Phillips*? *Maersk Alabama*
102. What is the third-largest land mammal? Hippopotamus
103. What is Velma's last name in *Scooby-Doo*? Dinkley
104. Who succeeded John Wooden as UCLA head men's basketball coach? Gene Bartow
105. In what state was oil first discovered in the United States? Pennsylvania
106. Kiwi birds are native to what country? New Zealand
107. What was Arthur's last name on *The King of Queens*? Spooner
108. What is the most widely consumed psychoactive drug? Caffeine
109. What is the real name of the woman in the picture of "Afghan Girl" on the November's 1985 cover of *National Geographic*? Sharbat Gula
110. Who plays Yondu in the *Guardians of the Galaxy* film franchise? Michael Rooker
111. What conference marked the only meeting between Harry Truman and Joseph Stalin? Potsdam Conference
112. What is the land of giants called in *Gulliver's Travels*? Brobdingnag
113. What Major League Baseball team drafted Tom Brady in the 1995 MLB Draft? Montreal Expos
114. What famous book that was first published in 1931 did Irma Rombauer write? *The Joy of Cooking*
115. In what city is the Van Gogh Museum located? Amsterdam, Netherlands
116. What was the first boxing match available on pay-per-view? Thrilla in Manila

117. Glycine max is more commonly known by what name? Soybean
118. Who was the judge for the court case People v. O.J. Simpson? Lance Ito
119. What major international event occurred on April 26, 1986? Chernobyl Disaster
120. What was the last NBA team that Shaquille O'Neal player for? Boston Celtics
121. If an employee works 8 hours a day, 5 days a week for 52 weeks, how many total hours will they work in a year? 2,080 hours
122. Whose first-person point of view tells the story in the book *Flowers in the Attic*? Cathy Dollanganger
123. The designation KV62 would lead to whose burial site? Tutankhamun
124. What was the first single released from *Thriller*? "The Girl is Mine"
125. What is the primary mineral that chalk is made of? Calcite
126. Who is the only member of the United States Coast Guard to have received the Medal of Honor? Douglas Munro
127. What is the smallest tiger subspecies? Sumatran tiger
128. At what temperature are the Fahrenheit and Celsius scales the same? -40 degrees
129. Toledo is the name of a city in what European country? Spain
130. Who did Pamela Courson find dead in their apartment on July 3, 1971? Jim Morrison
131. Phoebe is a satellite (moon) of what planet? Saturn
132. Suge Knight played for what NFL team during the 1987 NFL Strike? L.A. Rams
133. What was the code name for the top secret, CIA project to recover the Soviet submarine, *K-129*? Project Azorian
134. Ailurophobia is the fear of what? Cats

135. What space shuttle disintegrated upon re-entry on February 1, 2003? *Columbia*
136. What ship was discovered deserted and adrift off the Azores Islands on December 5, 1872? *Mary Celeste*
137. What 2004 movie is partly based on the book *Queen Bees and Wannabees*? *Mean Girls*
138. Where is the valley Taurus-Littrow located? The Moon
139. What is another name for Wardenclyffe Tower? Tesla Tower
140. What Rock and Roll Hall of Famer died on April 21, 2016? Prince
141. In what country are the Dolomites located? Italy
142. What African explorer changed his name from John Rowlands? Henry Morton Stanley
143. Who did Leonardo DiCaprio depict in *The Wolf of Wall Street*? Jordan Belfort
144. What is the primary protein found in human hair? Keratin
145. Who is the only two-time winner of the Nobel Prize in Physics? John Bardeen
146. What two countries does the Durand Line separate? Pakistan and Afghanistan
147. Where did the television show *Golden Girls* take place? Miami
148. What was the first jet fighter used by the United States military? P-59 Airacomet
149. Which amendment of the U.S. Constitution banned slavery? 13th Amendment
150. What is the most populous city in the Middle East? Cairo, Egypt
151. What was Disney's first full length animated film? *Snow White and the Seven Dwarfs*
152. Wars of the Diadochi followed what leader's death? Alexander the Great
153. What did Clyde Tombaugh discover in 1930? Pluto

154. Who painted *Guernica* in response to the bombing of Guernica? Pablo Picasso
155. In the comic strip *Calvin and Hobbes*, who is the inspiration for Hobbes? Thomas Hobbes
156. What football club does Liverpool play against in the Merseyside Derby? Everton
157. What type of cell does Sickle-Cell anemia affect? Red blood cell
158. What planet has the Great Dark Spot? Neptune
159. Who was the United States Army Corp of Engineers officer who oversaw and directed the Manhattan Project? Leslie Groves
160. Who is sometimes called, The Whitechapel Murderer? Jack the Ripper
161. What band opened their set at Woodstock '94 wearing lightbulb costumes? Red Hot Chili Peppers
162. What is the least awarded badge in the U.S. military? Astronaut badge
163. How many banks are in the United States Federal Reserve? 12
164. What superhero's alter ego is Princess Diana of Themyscira? Wonder Woman
165. What was rediscovered on July 14, 1986? *Titanic*
166. Who drew *Vitruvian Man*? Leonardo da Vinci
167. By what name was Mohawk leader Thayendanegea also known by? Joseph Brant
168. What is the name of the seamstress who dies from tuberculosis in *La bohème*? Mimi
169. What U.S. President signed the Uniform Code of Military Justice (UCMJ) into law? Harry Truman
170. What early Hollywood star said, "I believe in censorship? I made a fortune out of it"? Mae West
171. Who is the only American-born woman to receive full French military honors at her funeral? Josephine Baker

172. What is the name of the sculpture on the grounds of CIA headquarters that holds four encrypted messages? Kryptos
173. In what country is Bran Castle located? Romania
174. What university is home to Bodleian Library? University of Oxford
175. Who was the first American buried at Kremlin Wall Necropolis? John Reed
176. What is the 2nd most spoken language in the world? Spanish
177. Who did Clint Eastwood portray in *Escape from Alcatraz*? Frank Morris
178. In what year did the Spanish-American War occur? 1898
179. What conference was held in Brussels, Belgium during autumn of 1911? Solvay Conference
180. Who was the first person to the first person to win Academy Awards as director, producer, and screenwriter for the same film? Billy Wilder
181. In what movie did Beyoncé make her film debut? *Austin Powers in Goldmember*
182. What Jamaican born musician was killed during a home invasion on September 11, 1987? Peter Tosh
183. What was the first solar powered satellite, as well as the oldest manmade satellite still in orbit? Vanguard 1
184. What book and subsequent movie tells the story of Christopher McCandless's adventure and demise in Alaska? *Into the Wild*
185. Bonanza is a municipality of what country? Nicaragua
186. What element has the Periodic Table symbol, Hg? Mercury
187. Dungeness is a type of what crustacean? Crab
188. Who was assassinated in the Manhattan's Audubon Ballroom on February 21, 1965? Malcom X
189. What is the oldest federal cultural institution in the United States? Library of Congress
190. Snow, Nashi and Callery are all types of what fruit? Pear

191. What was the first #1 song in the United States to feature rap music? *Rapture* by Blondie
192. What is the largest church in the world? St. Peter's Basilica
193. Who was the third man to walk on the Moon? Pete Conrad
194. The “Cry of Dolores” signifies the start of what major event? Mexican War for Independence
195. What is the world’s largest breed of cattle? Chianina
196. What river does Marco Polo Bridge span across? Yongding river
197. What is the name of the boundary line that separates Earth’s atmosphere and outer space? Kármán line
198. What movie was incorrectly announced to have won the 2017 Academy Award for Best Picture? *La La Land*
199. What is the brightest star in Earth’s night sky? Sirius
200. How many electors comprise the Electoral College in the United States? 538
201. How old was Princess Diana when she married Prince Charles? 20
202. What is the mass of light? Zero
203. What two U.S. state capitals are the closest in distance to each other? Providence, RI and Boston, MA
204. Who did *MTV* rank as the Greatest MC of all-time in 2006? Jay-Z
205. What NFL team hosted Super Bowl 50? San Francisco 49ers
206. What country did the Derg rule during parts of the 1970’s and 80’s? Ethiopia
207. What is the largest species of fish? Whale shark
208. What kind of organism is fungus? Eukaryotic
209. Who are the names of Ironman’s mom and dad? Maria and Howard Stark
210. In what sport would you use a xistera? Jai alai

211. What was the name of the New York City house that served as the first U.S. Presidential Mansion? Samuel Osgood House
212. Where was Camp X-Ray located? Guantanamo Bay, Cuba
213. What U.S. President signed the first executive order? George Washington
214. Who was the losing starting quarterback in Super Bowl I? Len Dawson
215. What was the first name of Will's aunt in *The Fresh Prince of Bel Air*? Vivian
216. Who was John Cazale married to at the time of his death in 1978? Meryl Streep
217. What former company's bankruptcy filing is the largest in U.S. history? Lehman Brothers
218. What was the last northern U.S. state to abolish slavery? New Jersey
219. What country's largest island is Viti Levu? Republic of Fiji
220. What's does the amount of a bird's plumage refer to? Amount of feathers
221. What was the name of the oil rig that exploded in the Gulf of Mexico on April 20, 2010? Deepwater Horizon
222. What military facility would you be visiting if you were at Homey Airport? Area 51
223. In what U.S. state was Kentucky Fried Chicken founder Harland Sanders born? Indiana
224. What is the required minimum age to be a U.S. Representative? 25
225. What is rapper and singer Drake's birth name? Aubrey Drake Graham
226. Who was the first English king or queen to live in Buckingham Palace? Queen Victoria
227. Who did singer Trisha Yearwood marry in 2005? Garth Brooks
228. What is the national bird of Mexico? Golden eagle

229. Infantile paralysis is another name for what disease? Polio
230. What is the more common name for the religious movement, Religious Society of Friends? Quakers
231. What was Nielsen's most watched TV series for 2001-2002? *Friends*
232. What is the official currency of Australia? Australian dollar
233. Esperanto is a type of what? Language
234. What is *Marvel* superhero Daredevil's birth name? Matt Murdock
235. What were the first names of the comedy duo, Laurel and Hardy? Stan Laurel and Oliver Hardy
236. Khartoum is the capital of what country? Sudan
237. What professional wrestler is nicknamed Nature Boy? Ric Flair
238. What country is home to the Flanders region? Belgium
239. In what U.S. state did the James–Younger Gang originate? Missouri
240. What 1990's movie had the characters Patrick Verona, Chastity Church and Katarina Stratford? *10 Things I Hate About You*
241. In Western Christianity, on what day is All Saint's Day celebrated? November 1
242. In mythology, what is the cross between an eagle and a lion called? Griffin
243. Who was leader of the Khmer Rouge? Pol Pot
244. How many stars are on the flag for the People's Republic of China? 5
245. Carrauntoohil is the highest point on what island? Ireland
246. What country is the world's largest producer of mangos? India
247. Adar is a month on what calendar? Hebrew calendar
248. What film won the 1982 Academy Award for Best Visual Effects? *E.T. the Extra-Terrestrial*

249. What World War II era broadcaster with the nickname Lord Haw-Haw, was executed for treason in the United Kingdom? William Joyce
250. What was the name of the submarine commander for *Red October* in the Tom Clancy's, *The Hunt for Red October*? Marko Ramius
251. Convicted for the murder of her husband David Blakely, who was the last woman to be executed in the United Kingdom? Ruth Ellis
252. In what U.S. state was the Walloon language formally used in the northeast part of the state? Wisconsin
253. What fictional superhero is the alias for Wanda Maximoff? Scarlet Witch
254. Who was the first U.S. President to graduate from the United States Naval Academy? Jimmy Carter
255. Who was the last Major League Baseball player to wear jersey number 42? Mariano Rivera
256. What is the name of the Japanese dish in which soybeans are fermented with *Bacillus subtilis*? Nattō
257. What material would the Janka hardness test be used to classify? Wood
258. What late singer had the first #1 single on the *Billboard* Hot 100? Ricky Nelson (*Poor Little Fool*)
259. What is the minimum required age to become Prime Minister of the United Kingdom? 18 years old
260. *Torchwood* is a spin-off of what British television show? *Doctor Who*
261. What Grammy Award winning singer was born Stefani Joanne Angelina Germanotta? Lady Gaga
262. What U.S. President's grandson was the first baby born in the White House? Thomas Jefferson
263. What Latin word translates to, "Before the war"? Antebellum
264. What is O.J. Simpson's first name? Orenthal

265. In what country was House of Fabergé founded? Russia
266. What organization uses the abbreviation G.A.O.T.U? Freemasons (Great Architect of the Universe)
267. What American criminal was born Charles Milles Maddox? Charles Manson
268. Who played the angel Seth, in *City of Angels*? Nicholas Cage
269. What kind of animal is a Mexican howler? Monkey
270. What actress' 1991 autobiography is titled, *Little Girl Lost*? Drew Barrymore
271. What board game has the Murphy Rule? Backgammon
272. Who is the cover mascot for *Mad* magazine? Alfred E. Neuman
273. On what continent would you find Botany Bay? Australia
274. What was the largest tropical cyclone ever recorded? Typhoon Tip
275. Who became Acting President of Russia on December 31, 1999? Vladimir Putin
276. In what African country did the Mau Mau Uprising occur? Kenya
277. On what island does Mount Etna sit? Sicily
278. What is the last name of the three sister witches in the movie *Hocus Pocus*? Sanderson
279. What organization did Peter Benenson found in 1961? Amnesty International
280. What musician was born Herbert Buckingham Khaury in 1932? Tiny Tim
281. What is Quagmire's first name on *Family Guy*? Glenn
282. What singer's debut album spent the most weeks on the charts during the 2000's? Taylor Swift
283. In Greek mythology, who was the first King of Crete? Minos
284. What is the second most-visited house in the United States? Graceland

285. What was the halftime score of Super Bowl LI (51)? Atlanta Falcons 21, New England Patriots 3
286. What is the longest criminal jury trial in U.S. federal courts history? Pizza Connection Trial
287. What music producer developed the Wall of Sound? Phil Spector
288. In what 2001 movie did Tony Robbins guest star? *Shallow Hal*
289. What world city has the nickname, Big Smoke? London, England
290. Who played the role of Lestat in *Interview with the Vampire*? Tom Cruise
291. On what river does Hanoi, Vietnam sit? Red River
292. What band did Axl Rose become lead singer of in 2016? AC/DC
293. What bird has the longest beak? Australian pelican
294. What is singer Adele's maiden last name? Adkins
295. What 1982 movie was based on the novel, *Do Androids Dream of Electric Sheep? Blade Runner*
296. How many pints equal one peck? 16
297. What is the French sculpture *Le Penseur* known as in English? *The Thinker*
298. Who composed the violin concertos known as *The Four Seasons*? Vivaldi
299. How many codons make up the genetic code? 64
300. At what zoo did Harambe live his death? Cincinnati Zoo
301. In what game might someone use the Grünfeld Defence? Chess
302. Which planet in the Solar System has the strongest gravitational pull? Jupiter
303. What television show was based in the fictional town of Stars Hollow, Connecticut? *Gilmore Girls*
304. Who wrote the 1899 book, *The Interpretation of Dreams*? Sigmund Freud

305. What is the Roman numeral for 2025? MMXXV
306. Who did Ronda Rousey lose her first professional MMA fight to? Holly Holm
307. What current Russian city was once named Leningrad? Saint Petersburg
308. Who was the first Roman Emperor captured as a prison of war? Valerian
309. Who was the first American rock band to perform an open-air concert in Cuba? Audioslave
310. What is the world's main source of aluminum? Bauxite
311. What color is a Welsh poppy? Yellow
312. Who was the shortest U.S. President in history? James Madison
313. Who did singer Katy Perry marry in 2010? Russell Brand
314. Who developed the three Laws of Motion? Isaac Newton
315. What artist is Vincent van Gogh said to have had an argument with prior to partially cutting off his left ear? Paul Gauguin
316. What band released the album *Dookie* in 1994? Green Day
317. What is the oldest Major League Baseball club to never win the World Series? Texas Rangers
318. In welding, what do the letters MIG stand for? Metal Inert Gas
319. What is the capital of Delaware? Dover
320. What was the first band to be inducted into the Songwriters Hall of Fame? Queen
321. How many official languages does the United Nations have? 6 (Arabic, Chinese, English, French, Russian and Spanish)
322. In what city is Luxembourg Palace and Garden located? Paris, France
323. What is Harry's last name in *Dumb and Dumber*? Dunne
324. What is the name of the blood of gods and immortals in Greek mythology? Ichor

325. What Giuseppe Verdi opera translates to *The Fallen Woman*? *La traviata*
326. In what year did the world's population reach 1 billion? 1804
327. How many U.S. Presidents were only children? Zero
328. How many days were the Chilean miners trapped in 2010 before being rescued? 69 days
329. In what city is the headquarters for Scotland Yard located? London, England
330. What is the largest single machine in the world? Large hadron collider
331. What is the world's largest tree-borne fruit? Jackfruit
332. As of the 2016 election, how U.S. Presidential elections has the U.S. had? 56
333. Who was the Deep Throat source during Watergate? Mark Felt
334. What English writer used the pen name, Ellis Bell? Emily Brontë
335. What was the name of the baby that appeared on the cover of the first *TV Guide* in 1953? Desi Arnaz Jr.
336. What was the name of the flag for the Confederate States of America? Bonnie Blue Flag
337. For what NFL team was actress Teri Hatcher a cheerleader for in the 1980's? San Francisco 49ers
338. What was the first Netflix original series? *House of Cards*
339. What was the year, make and model of the pickup on *Sanford and Son*? 1951 Ford F1
340. Who was the first author to write a novel entirely on a computer? Jerry Pournelle
341. What Disney character has appeared in the most films? Donald Duck
342. What university did Bruce Lee attend? University of Washington

343. What Fortune 500 company was originally called BackRub? Google
344. What was Honda's first production automobile? Honda T360
345. What is the seventh planet from the Sun? Uranus
346. What is the national animal of Scotland? Unicorn
347. Outside what New York City apartment building was John Lennon murdered in 1980? The Dakota
348. What was the name of the crime family that Tony Soprano was head of in *The Sopranos*? DiMeo crime family
349. What does an apiarist work with? Bees (beekeeper)
350. Sophophobia is the fear of what? Learning

Food & Beverages

Get in me belly

1. Long Island Cheese, Ghost Rider and Big Max are all varieties of what plant? Pumpkin
2. What organ from a pig is used to make chitlins? Small intestine
3. What kind of food is a shiitake? Mushroom
4. What type of pasta means "little tongues" in Italian? Linguine
5. What is the national dish of Hungary? Goulash
6. What type of liquid are ladyfingers dipped into when making tiramisu? Coffee
7. What root is the primary ingredient in borsch? Beetroot
8. Laura and King Edward are both types of what food crop? Potato
9. What are the four fine herbs of French cuisine? Tarragon, Parsley, Chervil, Chives
10. From what root is tapioca extracted? Cassava root
11. What company manufactures Guinness? Diageo
12. What type of cured meat is prosciutto? Ham
13. What type of wheat is used to make traditional Italian spaghetti? Durum wheat
14. Hogget meat comes from what animal? Sheep
15. What type of bulb is used to make aioli? Garlic
16. What type of beef steak is called a Scotch fillet in Australia? Ribeye
17. Bourbon whiskey is made from what fermented grain? Corn
18. What is removed from cow's milk to make condensed milk? Water
19. What type of fruit is used to make Eton mess? Strawberries

20. Spearmint is mixed with what other mint to make peppermint? Watermint
21. What type of fermentation process is used to make ale? Warm fermintation
22. Challah is a special type of what Jewish food? Bread
23. What substance is fermented to make mead? Honey
24. What type of steak is most commonly used to make chicken fried steak? Cube steak
25. What kind of dough is used to make baklava? Filo
26. What is another common name for an alligator pear? Avocado
27. What juice is need to make Hollandaise sauce? Lemon juice
28. Danish Samsø is a type of what food? Cheese
29. What flavor is Triple sec? Orange
30. What Sicilian dessert means "little tube"? Cannoli
31. In Iceland, what is hákarl the fermented meat of? Shark
32. What type of fish is a kipper? Herring
33. What mammal's milk is used to make Roquefort cheese? Sheep
34. What type of wine is mixed with gin to create a martini? Vermouth
35. What type of dough is used to make an éclair? Choux
36. Ugli fruit are native to what country? Jamaica
37. Tourtière is a type of what dish? Meat pie
38. Most soju is made in what country? South Korea
39. What type of raw fish is used to make gravlax? Salmon
40. What is the common name for Japanese horseradish? Wasabi
41. In what country did strudel originate? Austria
42. What American lobster dish is made with butter, cream and cognac? Lobster Newberg
43. What ingredient is always found in traditional paella? White rice
44. What shape is a traditional tandoori oven? Cylindrical

45. Which of the French mother sauces is a Mornay sauce? Béchamel sauce
46. What dish has a filet steak coated with pâté and duxelles? Beef Wellington
47. Rainier and Royal Ann are both types of what fruit? Cherry
48. What liquid is added to a Black Russian drink to make a White Russian? Cream
49. From what country did Havarti cheese originate? Denmark
50. What Mexican food ingredient or topping translates to "beak of rooster"? Pico de gallo
51. What cake is named for the French patron saint of bakers and pastry chefs? St. Honoré cake
52. What kind of bread is traditionally used to make a Reuben sandwich? Rye bread
53. What kind of fish is used to make Lomi-lomi? Salmon
54. In what fruit is the bromelain enzyme found? Pineapple
55. What type of edible fungus is Périgord, France known for? Truffles
56. What fruit is served on the side with an espresso Romano? Slice of lemon
57. What country are macadamia trees indigenous to? Australia
58. What raw piece of food would you drink if you had a prairie oyster? Raw egg
59. At what annual sporting event is the mint julep known for? Kentucky Derby
60. What type of food is cooked al dente (firm to the bite)? Pasta
61. What is the name of the Canadian dish that consists of French fries and cheese curds covered with brown gravy? Poutine
62. What is the state fruit of Idaho? Huckleberry
63. What fruit is primarily used to make Bigarade sauce? Orange
64. What is the hardest nut shell to crack? Macadamia nut
65. In what country is Barbancourt rum produced and bottled? Haiti
66. What nut is used to make marzipan? Almond

67. Bonnie Brae, Eureka and Sorrento are all varieties of what fruit? Lemon
68. What does the IPA acronym stand for on an IPA beer bottle? India Pale Ale
69. In what country did the noodle soup Pho originate? Vietnam
70. What kind of beverage is Kopi Luwak? Coffee
71. What is it called when you cut a zig-zag pattern around a lemon? Vandyke
72. How many tablespoons equal one cup? 16
73. What are the tiny balls inside Bubble tea made of? Tapioca
74. What is the most cultivated type of coffee bean? Arabica
75. What is another name for the edible fruit aubergine? Eggplant
76. What type of dish is ragout? Stew
77. What is the name of the Sardinian cheese that contains live maggots? Casu marzu
78. A *Radler* is a mix of beer and what sparkling beverage? Lemonade
79. What company introduced Spam in 1937? Hormel
80. Liberty cabbage is another name for what fermented food? Sauerkraut
81. The bottle of what brand of alcohol has a small growing cross set between the antlers of a stag? Jägermeister
82. Consommé is a type of what food dish? Soup
83. What is the primary ingredient of Kaymak? Milk
84. What type of fish is used to prepare a Bombay duck? Lizardfish
85. What dessert gets its name because it resembles a snow-capped mountain? Mount Blanc
86. What is a cluster of bananas called? Hand
87. Himalayan salt comes from what country? Pakistan
88. The oil from what type of orange is used to flavor Earl Grey tea? Bergamot
89. What vegetable is used to make a Florentine dish? Spinach

90. What fruit is used to make Calvados brandy? Apples
91. What type of pasta means "little ears"? Orecchiette
92. What wine is specific to the Douro Valley in Portugal? Port wine
93. What drink did John Glenn help make famous for taking into space in 1962? Tang
94. What juice is used to make a Piña colada? Pineapple
95. What California city hosts a large garlic festival? Gilroy, CA
96. What kind of "cheese" is also called brawn? Head cheese (not a real cheese)
97. Kelvedon Wonder and Mr. Big are both varieties of what vegetable? Pea
98. What spice comes from the Crocus plant? Saffron
99. What is the name of the pastry type that is a criss-crossing pattern of strips and often used on pies? Lattice
100. What is the first course of a formal Italian meal? Antipasto
101. The cinnamon roll is believed to have originated in what country? Sweden
102. What does a jeroboam hold? Wine
103. What kind of nut is also called a cobnut, or filbert nut? Hazelnut
104. What part of a pig is used to make the German dish Eisbein? Ham hock
105. What kind of cheese is used to make Crab Rangoon? Cream cheese
106. What kind of food is produced in an apiary? Honey
107. What does the acronym BPA stand for that is found on many plastic water bottles and food containers? Bisphenol A
108. Which day each year has the most American pizza deliveries? Day before Thanksgiving
109. In what country was Pez invented? Austria
110. The juice of what fruit is used to make Balsamic vinegar? Grape

111. What hot dog company holds an annual hot dog eating competition each Independence Day on Coney Island, NY? Nathan's
112. What kind of fruit is the Japanese Yubari King? Cantaloupe
113. What is the culinary name for the thymus or pancreas of a lamb or calf? Sweetbread
114. What is the name for the spring rolls you'd eat in the Philippines? Lumpia
115. What Scandinavian dish means "lye fish"? Lutefisk
116. What is the culinary term for poking holes or "needling" the muscle of meat? Jacquarding
117. What does a Veronique dish always contain? Grapes
118. What is the more common name for theobroma oil? Cocoa butter
119. What is it called to remove the outermost skin of an apple? Pare
120. What is the white, edible part of cauliflower called? Curd
121. What country is the world's largest producer of watermelon? China
122. What is the primary acid found in fruits such as pears, apples, and peaches? Malic acid
123. What fruit should you never eat or drink if taking birth control or an antibiotic? Grapefruit
124. What nut is used to make Nutella? Hazelnut
125. What is poured over ice cream or gelato to make an affogato? Espresso (hot)

Like Literature?

Between the Pages

1. Jenny Fields is the mother of what literary character that was played by Robin Williams in a movie based on the title character? T.S. Garp (*The World According to Garp*)
2. "Reader, I married him," is part of the conclusion to what Charlotte Bronte novel? *Jane Eyre*
3. What is Gulliver's first name in *Gulliver's Travels*? Lemuel
4. What is the name of the swan who has no voice, but plays the trumpet in *The Trumpet of the Swan*? Louis
5. *War and Peace* tells the stories of how many different Russian families? Five
6. Who wrote *Tarzan of the Apes*? Edgar Rice Burroughs
7. What book tells the story of George Milton and Lennie Small? *Of Mice and Men*
8. What was Oscar Wilde's only novel? *The Picture of Dorian Gray*
9. What did Jean Valjean steal to serve prison time in *Les Misérables*? Bread
10. Who is the second-oldest March sister in *Little Women*? Jo (Josephine)
11. Who wrote the *Discworld* book series? Terry Pratchett
12. What is the name of the record Holden Caulfield wants to buy for his sister Phoebe in *The Catcher in the Rye*? *Little Shirley Beans*
13. What novel is a first-person account of American Frederic Henry during World War I? *A Farewell to Arms*
14. Leopold Bloom is the hero in what famous novel set in Dublin, Ireland? *Ulysses*

15. Who wrote the poem "The Love Song of J. Alfred Prufrock"? T.S. Eliot
16. What is the name of the boy who is chosen to inherit Receiver of Memory in *The Giver*? Jonas
17. Who was the survivor of Auschwitiz that would later write *Man's Search for Meaning*? Viktor Frankl
18. What city is the setting for *Brave New World* by Aldous Huxley? London, England
19. *Requiem for a Nun* was the sequel to what William Faulkner novel? *Sanctuary*
20. What was the name of the unfinished F. Scott Fitzgerald novel that was published posthumously? *The Last Tycoon*
21. What is the name of the stepdaughter in *Lolita*? Dolores Haze
22. What writer developed Objectivism? Ayn Rand
23. George Beard and Harold Hutchins are main characters in what children's novel series? *Captain Underpants*
24. What is the husband's name who is accused of killing his wife in *Gone Girl*? Nick Dunne
25. Who is Katniss Everdeen's younger sister in *The Hunger Games* series? Primrose (Prim)
26. What poem did Robert Frost recite at President John F. Kennedy's inauguration? "The Gift Outright"
27. What 1962 book by Rachel Carson discussed the dangers of pesticides? *Silent Spring*
28. Whose autobiography is titled *Up from Slavery*? Booker T. Washington
29. Who was the first musician to win the Nobel Prize in Literature? Bob Dylan
30. What novel by World War I veteran Erich Maria Remarque was banned by Nazi Germany is titled *Im Westen nichts Neues* in German? *All Quiet on the Western Front*
31. The film *Stand by Me* is based on what Stephen King novella? *The Body*

32. Published in 1960, *The Colossus and Other Poems* was what poet's only volume of poetry published while they were still alive? Sylvia Plath
33. What British poet initially coined the phrased, "'Tis better to have loved and lost: Than never to have loved at all"? Alfred, Lord Tennyson
34. Walt Whitman's "When Lilacs Last in the Dooryard Bloom'd" is an elegy for what famous American? Abraham Lincoln
35. What is the name of the shepherd boy in Paulo Coelho's *The Alchemist*? Santiago
36. What playwright won the Pulitzer Prize for Drama posthumously for his play, *Long Day's Journey into Night*? Eugene O'Neill
37. Which of King Lear's three daughters was murdered? Cordelia
38. What is the name of Dr. Seuss' first children's book? *And to Think That I Saw It on Mulberry Street*
39. What is the last name of the children in *The Chronicles of Narnia* series? Pevensie
40. Mitchell McDeere is a main character in what John Grisham novel? *The Firm*
41. What American writer was born on July 19, 1809 in Boston, Massachusetts? Edgar Allan Poe
42. Who owned Walden Pond that Henry David Thoreau wrote about in *Walden*? Ralph Waldo Emerson
43. What musical instrument did Sherlock Holmes play in the stories by Sir Arthur Conan Doyle? Violin
44. What children's book tells the story of an orphan boy named James Trotter? *James and the Giant Peach*
45. In what young adult book would you find the character Stanley Yelnats IV? *Holes*
46. What city is the setting for Kathryn Stockett's novel, *The Help*? Jackson, Mississippi

47. During what war does *The Book Thief* take place? World War II
48. Who wrote *Looking for Alaska*? John Green
49. Who is the main character in *The Count of Monte Cristo*? Edmond Dantès
50. In what year was Harry Potter born? 1980
51. What nationality is Santiago in *The Old Man and the Sea*? Cuban
52. What is the name of the short story by Jack London about a man who freezes to death in the Yukon Territory? "To Build a Fire"
53. Who are the Greasers' rival group in *The Outsiders*? Socs (Socials)
54. In what New York mountain range did Rip Van Winkle sleep for 20 years? Catskills
55. What was the name of William Shakespeare's wife? Anne Hathaway
56. Who wrote "The Ugly Duckling"? Hans Christian Andersen
57. What author's final work is *Finnegans Wake*? James Joyce
58. What two cities are the basis for *A Tale of Two Cities*? Paris and London
59. What is the boy's first name in *Where the Wild Things Are*? Max
60. What fictional character was born Max Eisenhardt? Magneto
61. What city is the primary setting for *On the Beach*? Melbourne, Australia
62. Big Daddy and Big Mama are characters in what Tennessee Williams play? *Cat on a Hot Tin Roof*
63. What novel introduced the word "Grok"? *Stranger in a Strange Land*
64. What is the best-selling novel of all-time? *Don Quixote*
65. *A Moveable Feas*t is a memoir by what late Nobel Laureate? Ernest Hemingway

66. What novel tells the story of an architect named Howard Roark? *The Fountainhead*
67. What is Algernon in *Flowers for Algernon*? A mouse
68. What was the first winner of the Nebula Award for Best Novel? *Dune*
69. Who was Scarlett O'Hara's first husband in *Gone with the Wind*? Charles Hamilton
70. Who is the only writer to have won Pulitzer Prizes for both poetry and fiction? Robert Penn Warren
71. Who wrote *The Wonderful World of Oz*? L. Frank Baum
72. What 1973 book by Flora Rheta Schreiber tells the true story of Shirley Ardell Mason? *Sybil*
73. In what book does Guy Montag work as a "fireman" who burns books? *Fahrenheit 451*
74. What is the name of the seamstress who has a baby named Pearl in *The Scarlett Letter*? Hester Prynne
75. What 1995 book by Steven Pressfield and later made into a film is loosely based on the *Bhagavad Gita*? *The Legend of Bagger Vance: A Novel of Golf and the Game of Life*

Famous People You Might Remember

Some you'll know

1. What German philosopher wrote *The World as Will and Representation*? Arthur Schopenhauer
2. Who is called the "Wizard of Menlo Park"? Thomas Edison
3. What French monarch was succeeded by his five-year-old great-grandson? Louis XIV
4. Who made the first public radio broadcast in 1906? Reginald Fessenden
5. Who was owner of the first electrically lit private residence in New York City? J.P. Morgan
6. What is the name of the Secret Service agent who was driving the limousine that President John F. Kennedy was riding in when he was assassinated? William Greer
7. Who founded the Franciscan Order? Saint Francis of Assisi
8. What Middle East leader was assassinated on October 6, 1981? Anwar Sadat
9. Who was Secretary of Defense during the Iran-Contra affair? Caspar Weinberger
10. Who choreographed the ballet *Deuce Coupe*? Twyla Tharp
11. Who founded the Carolingian dynasty? Charles Martel
12. Who authored the 1889 article "The Gospel of Wealth"? Andrew Carnegie
13. Who wrote the all-female play *The Women* and was later U.S. Ambassador to Italy and Brazil? Clare Boothe Luce
14. Who was the first President of Gran Colombia? Simón Bolívar

15. Who was the only sitting member of the U.S. House of Representatives to have been assassinated in office? Leo Ryan
16. Who is the only U.S. President to be awarded the Medal of Honor? Theodore Roosevelt
17. Who was U.S. Secretary of Defense at the start of the Vietnam War? Robert McNamara
18. By what name is Jorge Mario Bergoglio better known? Pope Francis
19. Who was the only First Lady born outside of the United States? Louisa Adams
20. Who was Flight Director for the Apollo 13 mission? Gene Kranz
21. Who attempted to assassinate President Ronald Reagan on March 30, 1981? John Hinckley Jr.
22. Who is the youngest-ever Vice President of the United States? John C. Breckinridge
23. Who was the first President of the Russian Federation? Boris Yeltsin
24. Who was King of the United Kingdom when Winston Churchill first became Prime Minister? George VI
25. Who founded Providence Plantations in present-day Rhode Island? Roger Williams
26. Who founded the Academy in Athens? Plato
27. Who is the only person to have been featured on the U.S. ten-dollar bill who only served in the military and never in politics? General Philip Sheridan
28. Who was the first female ambassador in European history? Catherine of Aragon
29. What former member of the Manson family was nicknamed Squeaky and attempted to assassinate President Gerald Ford? Lynette Fromme

30. Who commanded the 7th Cavalry Regiment when they were defeated at the Battle of Little Bighorn? George Armstrong Custer
31. Who was the first African American to win the Nobel Peace Prize? Ralph Bunche
32. What Roman Emperor ended the persecution of Christians? Constantine the Great
33. Who was the first person to circumnavigate the world as captain while leading the expedition throughout the entire voyage? Francis Drake
34. Who was the first president of the Southern Christian Leadership Conference? Martin Luther King Jr.
35. Who is the only person to win the Medal of Honor, the Distinguished Service Cross, the Distinguished Service Medal, and the National Security Medal? William Donovan
36. What is the name of the Dutch exotic dancer who was executed by France in 1917 for being a German spy? Mata Hari
37. Which of King Henry VIII's wives gave birth to King Edward VI? Jane Seymour
38. Who was the first Chief Justice of the United States? John Jay
39. What was the name of the professional tennis player who survived the sinking of the *Titanic* and would later win the U.S. Open? R. Norris Williams
40. Who was the last wife of Napoleon Bonaparte? Marie Louise
41. After Winston Churchill, who was the second person to be named an Honorary Citizen of the United States? Raoul Wallenburg
42. Who was the founder of psychoanalysis? Sigmund Freud
43. Who was coronated King of Scots on March 25, 1306? Robert the Bruce (Robert I)
44. Who was the first person to die at the Berlin Wall? Ida Siekmann

45. What African ruler was born Tafari Makonnen Woldemikael in 1892? Haile Selassie
46. Who won the 1983 Nobel Peace Prize and was also the leader of Solidarity in Poland? Lech Walesa
47. What is the name of the Pima Native American who was one of the six Americans to raise the American flag over Mount Suribachi on Iwo Jima? Ira Hayes
48. Who was the first U.S. military officer to be appointed to the grade of lieutenant general? George Washington
49. Who was the first Prime Minister of Canada? John Macdonald
50. What U.S. President married the widow Martha Wayles Skelton? Thomas Jefferson
51. Who was the first woman to receive a medical degree in the United States? Elizabeth Blackwell
52. Who translated the first Bible that was printed using the printing press? William Tyndale
53. Who was the only U.S. Army officer to have been promoted to General of the Armies while he was still alive? John "Black Jack" Pershing
54. Who carried out the 1972 assassination attempt on U.S. Presidential candidate George Wallace? Arthur Bremer
55. Who signed for the U.S. on board USS *Missouri* when Japan surrendered to end World War II? Admiral Chester Nimitz
56. Who was awarded the 1922 Nobel Prize in Physics? Niels Bohr
57. Who was the first President of the Continental Congress? Peyton Randolph
58. Who was the last British monarch from House of Hanover? Queen Victoria
59. Who divided the Bible into its current standard arrangement of chapters? Stephen Langton
60. Who did Marina Nikolayevna marry in 1961? Lee Harvey Oswald

61. Who has been the only major mob boss to receive the death penalty in the United States? Louis Buchalter
62. What winner of the Noble Peace Prize co-founded Hull House? Jane Addams
63. Who served the shortest term as an Associate Justice of the United States Supreme Court? John Rutledge
64. Who was the first American to be acquitted using temporary insanity as a legal defense? Daniel Sickles
65. Who was the last Communist leader of East Germany? Egon Krenz
66. Who was Ronald Reagan's first wife? Jane Wyman
67. Which Pope called for the Fourth Crusade? Pope Innocent III
68. Who was the voice of Underdog in the original cartoon series? Wally Cox
69. Who wrote *The Gulag Archipelago*? Aleksandr Solzhenitsyn
70. Who is the official State Hero of Connecticut? Nathan Hale
71. What actor or actress has the most Emmy Award wins in an acting role? Chloris Leachman (8)
72. Who was the last wife of Julius Caesar? Calpurnia
73. What Spanish conquistador was the first European to cross the Mississippi River? Hernando de Soto
74. What mobster and leader of Murder Inc., was nicknamed The Mad Hatter? Albert Anastasia
75. Who was the first non-European to hold the position of Secretary-General of the United Nations? U Thant
76. Who succeeded Adolf Hitler as Chancellor of Germany for just one day before he committed suicide? Joseph Goebbels
77. Who was the first Great Royal Wife of Ramses II? Nefertari
78. Who served on active duty as a U.S. general longer than anyone in history? Winfield Scott
79. Who wrote *Utopia* and was later tried for treason and beheaded by King Henry VIII? Thomas More
80. Who founded the political party Fatah? Yasser Arafat

81. Who received the Medal of Honor for his heroism during World War II at Colmar Pocket (France)? Audie Murphy
82. Who replaced John Dillinger as the FBI's Public Enemy Number One? Baby Face Nelson
83. Who holds the record as the longest serving Navy officer in U.S. history? Admiral Hyman Rickover
84. What leader did Leon Czolgosz assassinate in 1901? U.S. President William McKinley
85. What spy had the wartime codename, Intrepid? William Stephenson
86. Who hosted the Academy Awards a record 19 times? Bob Hope
87. Who was the longest serving Prime Minister of Britain during the 20th Century? Margaret Thatcher
88. Who was slated to be command pilot of Apollo 1 before a fire killed the three crew members during a launch rehearsal? Virgil "Gus" Grissom
89. Who founded the French Fifth Republic? Charles de Gaulle
90. What assassinated Martin Luther King Jr.? James Earl Ray
91. Who was the accused Soviet spy that was convicted of perjury in 1950? Alger Hiss
92. Who co-authored *The Communist Manifesto* with Karl Marx? Friedrich Engels
93. Who was the late American writer that said to "Follow your bliss" and wrote *The Hero with a Thousand Faces*? Joseph Campbell
94. Who was the first female to head a Muslim majority nation? Benazir Bhutto
95. Who painted *Portrait of Daniel-Henry Kahnweiler*? Pablo Picasso
96. What British general surrendered at Yorktown to end the American Revolutionary War? Charles Cornwallis
97. What retired NBA player scored 60 points during his final game on April 13, 2016? Kobe Bryant

98. What American gangster, who along with his gang, kidnapped Charles F. Urschel in 1933? Machine Gun Kelly
99. By what name is Joaquín Archivaldo Guzmán Loera better known by? El Chapo
100. Who was the only American soldier to be court-martialed and executed for desertion during World War II? Eddie Slovik

Screen Time

A mix of television and movies

1. In 2003 the American Film Institute named the Top 100 heroes and villains. What was the highest female villain? Wicked Witch of the West
2. What TV show revolved around the residents of Rome, Wisconsin? *Picket Fences*
3. After *Star Wars*, what was the 2nd highest-grossing-film of 1977? *Smokey and the Bandit*
4. What 1950's TV show is sometimes referred to as the "Classic 39"? *The Honeymooners*
5. In what state did the Walsh family live before moving to Beverly Hills in *Beverly Hills, 90210*? Minnesota
6. What was the only *Melrose Place* character to stay on for the show's entire run? Dr. Michael Mancini
7. In what movie was Rock Hudson captain of the fictitious submarine USS *Tigerfish*? *Ice Station Zebra*
8. What was the first known murder shown on live television? Jack Ruby shooting Lee Harvey Oswald
9. In *Friends*, what was the name of the character who moved in with Chandler for a brief time after Joey got his own apartment? Eddie
10. What was the first TV series broadcast over the internet? *Rox*
11. What were the names of the twin boys on *Everybody Loves Raymond*? Michael and Geoffrey
12. What was Newman's occupation on *Seinfeld*? U.S. Mailman
13. What was the first film to win eleven Academy Awards? *Ben-Hur* (1959)

14. What Academy Award winning actor was born on May 26, 1907 in Winterset, Iowa? John Wayne
15. What was the first of Shakespeare's plays to be adapted into a film? *King John* (1899)
16. On *Growing Pains*, who played Carol's boyfriend Sandy? Matthew Perry
17. In *Planes, Trains and Automobiles*, what does John Candy's character Del Griffith sell to make money? Shower curtain rings
18. What was the first movie that Will Ferrell and Mark Wahlberg both co-starred in together? *The Other Guys*
19. What movie was loosely based on the FBI's ABSCAM operation? *American Hustle*
20. What airline did Ray demand to fly aboard on *Rain Man*? Qantas
21. What was the name of the human little girl in *Monsters, Inc.*? Boo
22. Who provided the voice of Robin Masters in *Magnum P.I.*? Orson Welles
23. Who was an executive producer for both *Charlie's Angels* and *Dynasty*? Aaron Spelling
24. What was Dexter's last name in the television show *Dexter*? Morgan
25. What television show partly centered around the happenings at the Williamsburg Diner? *2 Broke Girls*
26. In the original *Knight Rider*, what does the acronym for Michael Knight's car KITT stand for? Knight Industries Two Thousand
27. What movie tells the true story of Frank Abagnale? *Catch Me If You Can*
28. What movie was Bruce Lee filming when he died? *Game of Death*
29. Who directed *The Dark Knight* (2008)? Christopher Nolan

30. In what movie did Goldie Hawn play a high school football coach? *Wildcats*
31. What character would regularly sleep off being drunk in Mayberry's jail on *The Andy Griffith Show*? Otis Campbell
32. Who was the first U.S. President to appear on television? Franklin D. Roosevelt
33. What state did Daniel and his mom move to California from in *The Karate Kid*? New Jersey
34. Who played the dad in *My Three Sons*? Fred MacMurray
35. What was the name of the flying Winnebago in *Spaceballs*? Eagle 5
36. On *The Simpsons*, what is Marge's maiden name? Bouvier
37. What is the name of the 1992 movie in which a former hockey player teams up with a female figure skater to compete in pairs figure skating? *The Cutting Edge*
38. What was the name of Doc Brown's dog in *Back to the Future*? Einstein
39. In what television series was Rebecca Howe infatuated with Evan Drake? *Cheers*
40. What was the name of the kidnapped dolphin in *Ace Ventura*? Snowflake
41. The character Arthur Carlson was general manager of what radio station? WKRP
42. The Peter Venkman character in *Ghostbusters* was originally written for what late actor? John Belushi
43. What was the first film starring The Beatles? *A Hard Day's Night*
44. What television show character created the persona, Grandmaster B? Bud Bundy
45. What is the son's name in *The Shining*? Danny Torrance
46. What television series was *Private Practice* a spin-off of? *Greys Anatomy*
47. What movie character said, "As God is my witness, as God is my witness they're not going to lick me"? Scarlett O'Hara

48. In what movie did Val Kilmer wear a gold Elvis suit? *True Romance*
49. What year were the Harley Davidson's that the main characters in *Easy Rider* rode? 1962
50. What was the name of the college the fraternity brothers attended in *Animal House*? Faber College
51. What was the first movie to sell one million copies on home video? *Dirty Dancing*
52. What was the first Vietnam War film made by a Vietnam War veteran? *Platoon*
53. What movie is based on a man's dying word of, "Rosebud"? *Citizen Kane*
54. Who has won the most (4) Academy Awards for Best Director? John Ford
55. *Diagnosis Murder* was a spin-off of what legal drama television show? *Matlock*
56. What U.S. President did Parker Sawyers depict in *Southside with You*? Barack Obama
57. In what movie is the title character's ex-girlfriend Stacy referred to as a "psycho hose-beast"? *Wayne's World*
58. What was the name of the high school that Richie and Potsie attended in *Happy Days*? Jefferson High
59. What is the name of the convenience store in *Clerks*? Quick Stop
60. What was the original title of *Return of the Jedi* before George Lucas changed it? Revenge of the Jedi
61. In what 1980's television show was it illegal to turn off your TV? *Max Headroom*
62. What was the name of Sonny Crockett's pet alligator on *Miami Vice*? Elvis
63. Who provided the narration in the movie *Tombstone*? Robert Mitchum
64. What TV series starred Jason Segel, James Franco and Linda Cardellini? *Freaks and Geeks*

65. In *Family Guy*, what is Chris' full name? Christopher Cross Griffin
66. What does the license plate for Cameron's father's Ferrari read in *Ferris Bueller's Day Off*? NRVOUS
67. In what movie do Patrick Dempsey and Brendan Fraser play students attending Harvard? *With Honors*
68. Who played Papa Elf in *ELF*? Bob Newhart
69. Who directed *Caddyshack*? Harold Ramis
70. What is the first name of the stripper that Stu married in *The Hangover*? Jade
71. In what film was Robin Williams nominated for the Academy Award for Best Actor for his character, John Keating? *Dead Poets Society*
72. What was the name of the woman Gary and Wyatt created in *Weird Science*? Lisa
73. In what movie did the mom and dad relocate to Earth from the planet Remulak? *Coneheads*
74. What was the name of the Brady's family dog on *The Brady Bunch*? Tiger
75. What clothing brand did Jeff Spicoli help make famous in *Fast Times at Ridgemont High*? Vans
76. What 1986 film was originally titled, "The Body"? *Stand By Me*
77. What was the final movie Stanley Kubrick produced and directed? *Eyes Wide Shut*
78. What was the first name of Cousin Eddie and Catherine's son in *National Lampoon's Christmas Vacation*? Rocky
79. In *Cool Hand Luke*, what song did Paul Newman play on the banjo? "Plastic Jesus"
80. In *Major League*, what was the name of the idol that Pedro Cerrano worshiped? Jobu
81. What character did Jennifer Garner play in *Alias*? Sydney Bristow

82. What was the name of Captain Malcolm Reynolds' ship on *Firefly*? Serenity
83. In what television series did Donald Trump have a cameo in 1985? *The Jeffersons*
84. What character did Paul Newman supply the voice to in *Cars*? Doc Hudson
85. What movie character originally said, "A boy's best friend is his mother"? Norman Bates (*Psycho*)
86. What state is Penny originally from in *The Big Bang Theory*? Nebraska
87. In *The Big Lebowski*, The Dude says that he was a roadie for what heavy metal band? Metallica
88. What is the name of the frontier town in *Blazing Saddles*? Rock Ridge
89. What university did Doogie Howser graduate from at the age of 10? Princeton
90. What actress played Berta's 16-year-old granddaughter in an episode of *Two and a Half Men*? Megan Fox
91. On *Seinfeld*, what kind of car did George buy thinking it had belonged to actor Jon Voight? Convertible Chrysler Le Baron
92. What was the name of the morning show that Danny and Rebecca co-hosted on *Full House*? Wake Up, San Francisco
93. David Prowse played the physical form of what famous movie character? Darth Vader
94. What was Anthony Edwards' character's call-sign in *Top Gun*? Goose
95. What was the name of the tree the *Gummi Bears* lived in? Gummi Glen
96. In what television series did John Ritter and Katey Sagal play Kaley Cuoco's parents? *8 Simple Rules for Dating My Teenage Daughter*
97. What fictional town was the setting for *Northern Exposure*? Cicely, Alaska

98. *Booker* was a spin-off of what television series? *21 Jump Street*
99. What is the name of the World War II era soccer movie Sylvester Stallone co-starred in? *Victory*
100. What is the first letter of all the sisters' names in *Charmed*? P
101. Who was the first storyteller of *Thomas the Tank Engine & Friends*? Ringo Starr
102. In *Raiders of the Lost Ark*, at what fictitious college is Indiana Jones a professor? Marshall College
103. What television show helped launch the career of Alanis Morissette? *You Can't Do That on Television*
104. Who did Sigourney Weaver portray in the film *Gorillas in the Mist*? Dian Fossey
105. For what film did both Jane Fonda and Jon Voight both win Academy Awards? *Coming Home*
106. On *Cheers*, what did Norm do for a profession after he quit being an accountant? Housepainter
107. Who played Kim in *Edward Scissorhands*? Winona Ryder
108. Who played Jeannie on *I Dream of Jeannie*? Barbara Eden
109. Who played Rachel's sister Jill on *Friends*? Reese Witherspoon
110. What is the name of the high school Zack and Screech attend in *Saved by the Bell*? Bayside High School
111. What was the name of the school that Walter White taught chemistry at in *Breaking Bad*? J. P. Wynne High School
112. What was Dwayne Johnson's first movie? *The Mummy Returns*
113. What was Mikey and Brand's last name in *The Goonies*? Walsh
114. What was the first name of D.J., Stephanie and Michelle's late mom on *Full House*? Pam
115. What city is the setting for *Lost in Translation*? Tokyo

116. What was the first name of Robert's second wife on *Everybody Loves Raymond*? Amy
117. What was Marlon Brando's final movie? *The Score*
118. What was the name of the store that Andy works at in *40-Year-Old Virgin*? Smart Tech
119. What is the last name of the superhero family in *The Incredibles*? Parr
120. What was the princess' name in *Spaceballs*? Princess Vespa
121. Who was the original announcer of the cast and guests *on Saturday Night Live*? Don Pardo
122. The filming of what Marilyn Monroe and Laurence Olivier film was part of the plot in *My Week with Marilyn*? *The Prince and the Showgirl*
123. *The Jeffersons* was a spin-off of what 1970's TV show? *All in the Family*
124. The title of what TV show was inspired from a U2 song? *One Tree Hill*
125. What film and TV franchise did Gene Roddenberry create? *Star Trek*

The Performing Arts

Musicals, ballets and the opera

1. In what country did ballet first originate? Italy
2. The musical *My Fair Lady* is based on what play by George Bernard Shaw? *Pygmalion*
3. What is the name of the shoe that a ballerina wears? Pointe
4. What opera tells the story of Swanhilda, Franz and a life-size dancing doll? *Coppélia*
5. What biographical musical did Clint Eastwood adapt into a 2014 film? *Jersey Boys*
6. The character Caino is a clown in what opera? *Pagliacci*
7. What musical was adapted into a movie that starred Marlon Brando, Frank Sinatra and Jean Simmons? *Guys and Dolls*
8. What is the name for a male dancer in a ballet company? Danseur
9. Cio-Cio-san is the main character in what opera? *Madama Butterfly*
10. Who wrote the song “The Music of the Night” from *The Phantom of the Opera*? Andrew Lloyd Webber
11. What is a slow dance movement in ballet called? Adagio
12. What is the name of the flower shop in *Little Shop of Horrors*? Mushnik's Skid Row Florists
13. What is the name of the princess who is turned into a swan in *Swan Lake*? Odette
14. At what ballet would you hear, "Dance of the Sugar Plum Fairy"? *The Nutcracker*
15. What musical is often associated with John F. Kennedy? *Camelot*

16. What rock opera has the song "I Don't Know How to Love Him"? *Jesus Christ Superstar*
17. The Wilis are prominent in what popular romantic ballet? *Giselle*
18. What musical's main female character is the Navy nurse Nellie Forbush? *South Pacific*
19. Gypsy Rose Lee's memoirs were the basis for what musical? *Gypsy*
20. What country is the setting for the opera, *Aida*? Egypt
21. Who played Elphaba in the original Broadway cast of *Wicked*? Idina Menzel
22. What is the name for the German system that is used to classify the voices of opera singers? *Fach*
23. What Igor Stravinsky ballet tells the story of three puppets? *Petrushka*
24. What is the name of the opera term for the "first lady" or female lead in an opera cast? Prima Donna
25. What musical is based on Jim Jacobs' time at William Howard Taft High School in Chicago? *Grease*
26. *Rent* is based on what Puccini opera? *La bohème*
27. What was the first opera performed in the United States? *Flora*
28. What is the name for the text used in an opera? Libretto
29. What ballerina danced the role of Clara Stahlbaum in the 1977 televised production of *The Nutcracker*? Gelsey Kirkland
30. What opera is set in Charleston, South Carolina and has the characters Crown and Sportin' Life? *Porgy and Bess*
31. In what Andrew Lloyd Webber rock musical does a train set come to life? *Starlight Express*
32. The "Bridal Chorus" is a famous part of what Richard Wagner opera? *Lohengrin*
33. What playwright created *Hamilton: An American Musical*? Lin-Manuel Miranda

34. In what musical is main character Dolly Levi a matchmaker? *Hello, Dolly!*
35. What ballet tells the story of Anna Anderson? *Anastasia*
36. What actor both wrote and performed the one-man play *A Bronx Tale*? Chazz Palminteri
37. What is the name of the ballet term for a dance done with four dancers? Pas de quatre
38. What Mel Brooks musical did Matthew Broderick and Nathan Lane both star in? *The Producers*
39. What Latvian born ballet dancer was nominated for an Academy Award for his role in *The Turning Point*? Mikhail Baryshnikov
40. What is the name of the tribe of cats in the musical, *Cats*? Jellicles
41. What is the highest female voice type in opera? Soprano
42. What musical holds the record as the longest-running American musical in Broadway history? *Chicago*
43. What Shakespearean play was the inspiration for *West Side Story*? *Romeo and Juliet*
44. What Stephen Sondheim musical tells the story of a Roman slave named Pseudolus who is trying to win his freedom? *A Funny Thing Happened on the Way to the Forum*
45. In what opera does Calaf sing the aria “Nessun dorma”? *Turandot*
46. What is the father’s name in *Fiddler on the Roof*? Tevye
47. Who played Sweeney Todd in the original 1979 Broadway cast of *Sweeney Todd: The Demon Barber of Fleet Street*? Len Cariou
48. Who is said to be the father of American ballet? George Balanchine
49. What musical was inspired by the Newsboys' strike of 1899? *Newsies*
50. What famous opera tells the story of a soldier named Don José? *Carmen*

Decades of the 80's & 90's

Relive the glory days and grunge era

1. What was the last name of the family ALF lived with on *ALF*? Tanner
2. What is the name of the 18-month old girl who was trapped in a well in Midland, Texas in 1987? Jessica McClure
3. What company produces Wayfarer sunglasses which were very popular in the 1980's? Ray-Ban
4. What is the name of the teenager from Indiana who was not allowed to attend school due to him having AIDS, and brought national attention to the disease after being befriended by Michael Jackson and Elton John? Ryan White
5. What hotel businesswoman was convicted of tax evasion and labeled the "Queen of Mean"? Leona Helmsley
6. On the TV show *A-Team*, what was the first name of B.A. Baracus? Bosco
7. What was the top grossing movie of the 80's? *E.T. the Extra-Terrestrial*
8. Who did Julia Roberts call off her engagement to in 1991? Kiefer Sutherland
9. What was Angela's mother's name in *Who's the Boss*? Mona Robinson
10. What alternative rock band featured Billy Corgan, James Iha and D'arcy Wretzky? The Smashing Pumpkins
11. Who was The Notorious B.I.G. married to at the time of his death? Faith Evans
12. Who played Caitlin on *Miami Vice*? Sheena Easton
13. Who released the *MTV* music video, "Lisa, Lisa, the One I Adore"? Pauly Shore

14. What was the top grossing movie of the 1990's? *Titanic*
15. Who played Miles in the movie *Uncle Buck*? Macaulay Culkin
16. What is the name of the retired soccer player Posh Spice married in 1999? David Beckham
17. What Seattle band's debut album was released in 1990 and titled *Facelift*? Alice in Chains
18. What musician did actress Heather Locklear marry in 1986? Tommy Lee
19. What fictional town is the setting for *Back to the Future*? Hill Valley, California
20. What #1 song from 1982 did the woman born Antonia Christina Basilotta have? "Mickey"
21. On what 1980's TV show did Jason Bateman play the friend Derek Taylor? *Silver Spoons*
22. Three Berggren siblings and Ulf Ekberg formed what popular 1990's group from Sweden? Ace of Base
23. What is the name of the then Washington D.C. mayor who was videotaped smoking crack cocaine in 1990? Marion Barry
24. What company had the "fast talker" TV commercials during the 1980's? Federal Express
25. What singer did Yolanda Saldívar murder in 1995? Selena
26. Who did J. Howard Marshall marry in 1994? Anna Nicole Smith
27. *Enos* was a spin-off of what famous 1980's TV show? *The Dukes of Hazzard*
28. From what city did the band A Flock of Seagulls originate from? Liverpool, England
29. Andrew Wood was the lead singer of what grunge rock band when he died of a heroin overdose? Mother Love Bone
30. What Hollywood actor was arrested in 1995 for being with Divine Brown? Hugh Grant

31. What actress did James Cameron divorce in 1997? Linda Hamilton
32. What NBC show did *Friends* follow when it debuted in 1994? *Mad About You*
33. What city was the setting for the movie *Singles*? Seattle
34. In what year was Nelson Mandela released from prison? 1990
35. What was the name of the benefit event that occurred on Sunday, May 25, 1986 in which millions of people held hands? Hands Across America
36. What famous couple were married on July 29, 1981? Prince Charles and Diana Spencer
37. Where was Jodie Foster attending college when John Hinkley attempted to assassinate Ronald Reagan? Yale University
38. In 1982, who became the first sitting member of Congress to go into outer space? Jake Garn?
39. Who said, "Win or lose, we go shopping after election"? Imelda Marcos
40. What was the name of the TV show in which gifted students were taught at a Manhattan high school and their history teacher was named Charlie Moore? *Head of the Class*
41. Who did singer Rod Stewart marry in 1990? Rachel Hunter
42. What jeans did Brooke Shields model in controversial commercials? Calvin Klein
43. In what city did the Tylenol murders of 1982 occur? Chicago, Illinois
44. Who were Freddie Helms and Bryant Allen passengers in a vehicle with when they were pulled over in California on March 3, 1991? Rodney King
45. What former stock broker who went to federal prison in the late 1980's for insider trading is the movie character Gordon Gekko loosely based on? Ivan Boesky
46. Who was dubbed the "Subway Vigilante" by the New York City media? Bernhard Goetz

47. Who was acknowledged as *Time* magazine's Man of the Decade for the 1980's? Mikhail Gorbachev
48. Who was the U.S. Marine Corps Lieutenant Colonel who was convicted during the Iran-Contra Affair? Oliver North
49. What supermodel starred in Pepsi's famous 1991 commercial? Cindy Crawford
50. What was Blossom's and Joey's last name on the TV show *Blossom*? Russo
51. Who was Kidada Jones engaged to when her fiancé was murdered in 1996? Tupac Shakur
52. What song did Bill Clinton play on the saxophone on *The Arsenio Hall Show* in 1992? "Heartbreak Hotel"
53. Who was Marcy married to after Steven Rhoades on *Married with Children*? Jefferson D'Arcy
54. What benefit concert did The Beastie Boys help organize in 1996? Tibetan Freedom Concert
55. What year was the World Series cancelled due to a strike? 1994
56. What TV show was *Empty Nest* a spin-off of? *The Golden Girls*
57. What is the name of the former Associated Press journalist who was abducted in Beirut on March 16, 1985 and held hostage by Hezbollah militants for over six years? Terry Anderson
58. Who had to withdraw her nomination as Attorney General of the United States in 1993 due to her role in Nannygate? Zoe Baird
59. What is the name of the former CIA agent who was arrested in 1994 and convicted of being a KGB mole? Aldrich Ames
60. What couple were on the January 22, 1981 cover of *Rolling Stone*? John Lennon and Yoko Ono
61. What band launched A Momentary Lapse of Reason Tour in 1987? Pink Floyd

62. What 1980 miniseries starred Richard Chamberlin as the character John Blackthorne? *Shōgun*
63. What city was the setting for *Mork & Mindy*? Boulder, CO
64. What was the first name of Kevin Arnold's brother on *The Wonder Years*? Wayne
65. On what soap opera did Luke and Laura get married? *General Hospital*
66. Who became boss of the Gambino crime family after he had Paul Castellano murdered? John Gotti
67. What U.S. city was one of the host cities for Live Aid in 1985? Philadelphia
68. Who did actress Robin Givens marry in 1988? Mike Tyson
69. What was the name of the NBC pilot George and Jerry wrote on *Seinfeld*? *Jerry*
70. What is the name of the woman who wrongly declared the winner of the 1980 Boston Marathon due to not running the entire race? Rosie Ruiz
71. What televangelist's scandal was Jessica Hahn a big part of? Jim Bakker
72. What late U.S. President's body was exhumed in 1991 to test for possible arsenic poisoning? Zachary Taylor
73. What Supreme Court nominee did Anita Hill accuse of past sexual harassment? Clarence Thomas
74. What duo reunited to play 1981's "The Concert in Central Park"? Simon & Garfunkel
75. What is the brothers' last name in *A Night at the Roxbury*? Butabi
76. Who was sentenced to death over the Oklahoma City bombing? Timothy McVeigh
77. Who did Bette Midler co-host the 1984 MTV Video Music Awards with? Dan Aykroyd
78. What is the name of the owl-looking toy first released in 1998 that could learn English? Furby

79. Who did Mr. T co-host a 1985 episode of *Saturday Night Live* with? Hulk Hogan
80. What is the name of the 1990's TV show that starred Jared Leto and Claire Danes? *My So-Called Life*
81. What was the name of the dojo that Kreese operated in *The Karate Kid*? Cobra Kai
82. Who played Uncle Ned on *Family Ties*? Tom Hanks
83. Who did Bjorn Bjorg defeat to win his fifth straight Wimbledon in 1980? John McEnroe
84. How many days were the American hostages held in Iran before their release in 1981? 444 days
85. Who was Walter Mondale's running mate in the 1984 U.S. Presidential election? Geraldine Ferraro
86. By what name is October 19, 1987 better known by? Black Monday (Stock Market Crash)
87. What was the family's last name in *Party of Five*? Salinger
88. What was the top grossing animated movie of the 1990's? *The Lion King*
89. Which doctor from *St. Elsewhere* contracted AIDS? Dr. Bobby Caldwell (Mark Harmon)
90. What TV show had the character Admiral Al Calavicci? *Quantum Leap*
91. What brand had the "New Neighbor" commercial starring Michael J. Fox? Diet Pepsi
92. In *Friends*, Joey played Dr. Drake Ramoray in what daytime soap opera? *Days of Our Lives*
93. Who was U.S. Vice President on January 1, 1990? Dan Quayle
94. What 1990's TV show had the next-door neighbor Mr. Wilson? *Home Improvement*
95. What NHL team won the first 4 Stanley Cup Finals of the 1980's? New York Islanders
96. Who did David marry in the series finale of *Beverly Hills, 90210*? Donna

97. Who did actor Tom Arnold marry in 1990? Roseanne Barr
98. Who made her debut on *American Bandstand* in 1982 singing "Young Love"? Janet Jackson
99. What 1980's toy line had the tag line of , "Loveable Huggable" and even had its own cartoon? Pound Puppies
100. What *Saturday Night Live* cast member portrayed Linda Richman in "Coffee Talk with Linda Richman"? Mike Myers

Who's the Oldest?

Which of the three was born first?

1. Galileo Galilei, Nicolaus Copernicus or Johannes Kepler? Nicolaus Copernicus
2. Alexander the Great, Julius Caesar or Marcus Aurelius? Alexander the Great
3. Franklin D. Roosevelt, Joseph Stalin or Winston Churchill? Winston Churchill
4. Grace Kelly, Audrey Hepburn or Marilyn Monroe? Marilyn Monroe
5. Richard Nixon, John F. Kennedy or Ronald Reagan? Ronald Reagan
6. Mickey Mantle, Hank Aaron or Willie Mays? Willie Mays
7. Greta Garbo, Katherine Hepburn or Bette Davis? Greta Garbo
8. Martin Luther King Jr., Nelson Mandela or Malcolm X? Nelson Mandela
9. Czar Nicholas II, Leon Trotsky or Vladimir Lenin? Nicholas II
10. Bruce Springsteen, Rod Stewart or Elton John? Rod Stewart
11. Marie Antoinette, Queen Victoria or Empress Joséphine? Marie Antoinette
12. Alexander Graham Bell, Thomas Edison or Nikola Tesla? Thomas Edison
13. Fidel Castro, Che Guevara or Robert F. Kennedy? Robert F. Kennedy
14. Douglas MacArthur, George Patton or Dwight D. Eisenhower? Douglas MacArthur
15. Amelia Earhart, Coco Chanel or Helen Keller? Helen Keller
16. Plato, Socrates or Aristotle? Socrates

17. Elvis Presley, Paul McCartney or Bob Dylan? Elvis Presley
18. John D. Rockefeller, Andrew Carnegie or J.P. Morgan? Andrew Carnegie
19. Claude Monet, Vincent van Gogh or Auguste Renoir? Claude Monet
20. J.R.R. Tolkien, C.S. Lewis or Ernest Hemingway? J.R.R. Tolkien
21. Joan of Arc, William Wallace or Kublai Khan? Kublai Khan
22. Bruce Lee, Chuck Norris or Harrison Ford? Chuck Norris
23. John Dillinger, Al Capone or J. Edgar Hoover? J. Edgar Hoover
24. Mark Twain, Oscar Wilde or Arthur Conan Doyle? Mark Twain
25. Charles Lindbergh, F. Scott Fitzgerald or Salvador Dali? F. Scott Fitzgerald
26. Ho Chi Minh, Mao Zedong or Adolf Hitler? Adolf Hitler
27. John Paul Jones, Horatio Nelson or John Paul Jones? John Paul Jones
28. Charles Darwin, Karl Marx or Henry David Thoreau? Charles Darwin
29. Henry VIII of England, Catherine the Great or Peter the Great? Henry VIII
30. Josephine Baker, Ella Fitzgerald or Billie Holiday? Josephine Baker
31. Christopher Columbus, Isaac Newton, or Michelangelo? Christopher Columbus
32. Janis Joplin, Jim Hendrix or Jim Morrison? Jimi Hendrix
33. Marie Curie, Niels Bohr or Erwin Schrödinger? Marie Curie
34. John Gotti, Bernie Madoff or Henry Hill? Bernie Madoff
35. Madonna, Cyndi Lauper or Pat Benatar? Pat Benatar

Book Quotes

Name the book for each quote

1. "Remember, we're madly in love, so it's all right to kiss me anytime you feel like it." *The Hunger Games*
2. "He was a silent fury who no torment could tame." *White Fang*
3. "When it came to gunfire Jumper didn't have any more sense than a red ant in a hot skillet." *Old Yeller*
4. "Guys like us got nothing to look ahead to." *Of Mice and Men*
5. "I would always rather be happy than dignified." *Jane Eyre*
6. "Freedom, like everything else, is relative." *The Handmaid's Tale*
7. "I'm quite illiterate, but I read a lot." *The Catcher in the Rye*
8. "The bird that would soar above the plain of tradition and prejudice must have strong wings." *The Hitchhiker's Guide to the Galaxy*
9. "This is your life and its ending one moment at a time." *Fight Club*
10. "The rebirth of the soul is perpetual; only rebirth every hour could stay the hand of Satan." *Go Tell It on the Mountain*
11. "The world breaks everyone and afterward many are strong at the broken places." *A Farewell to Arms*
12. "We took away your art because we thought it would reveal your souls. Or to put it more finely, we did it to prove you had souls at all." *Never Let Me Go*
13. "Friends see most of each other's flaws. Spouses see every awful last bit." *Gone Girl*
14. "And the walls became the world all around." *Where the Wild Things Are*
15. "The planet has survived everything, in its time. It will certainly survive us." *Jurassic Park*

16. "Those we love don't go away, they sit beside us every day." *Big Little Lies*
17. "It was not the feeling of completeness I so needed, but the feeling of not being empty." *Everything is Illuminated*
18. "We can't take any credit for our talents. It's how we use them that counts." *A Wrinkle in Time*
19. "It takes a great deal of bravery to stand up to our enemies, but just as much to stand up to our friends." *Harry Potter and the Sorcerer's Stone*
20. "When we love, we always strive to become better than we are. When we strive to become better than we are, everything around us becomes better too." *The Alchemist*
21. "I like the night. Without the dark, we'd never see the stars." *Twilight*
22. "May the wind under your wings bear you where the sun sails and the moon walks." *The Hobbit*
23. "She had waited all her life for something, and it had killed her when it found her." *Their Eyes Were Watching God*
24. "Come right up close to me and I will show you something wonderful." *James and the Giant Peach*
25. "Taking a new step, uttering a new word, is what people fear most." *Crime and Punishment*
26. "Like so many Americans, she was trying to construct a life that made sense from things she found in gift shops." *Slaughterhouse-Five*
27. "A person is, among all else, a material thing, easily torn and not easily mended." *Atonement*
28. "To choose doubt as a philosophy of life is akin to choosing immobility as a means of transportation." *Life of Pi*
29. "My thoughts are stars I cannot fathom into constellations." *The Fault in Our Stars*
30. "You have the freedom to be yourself, your true self, here and now, and nothing can stand in your way." *Jonathan Livingston Seagull*

31. “What are we? Humans? Or animals? Or savages?” *Lord of the Flies*
32. “You will always be fond of me. I represent to you all the sins you never had the courage to commit.” *The Picture of Dorian Gray*
33. “Write about what disturbs you, particularly if it bothers no one else.” *The Help*
34. “Kate Barlow died laughing.” *Holes*
35. “And all the lives we ever lived and all the lives to be are full of trees and changing leaves.” *To the Lighthouse*
36. “Trust me, Wilbur. People are very gullible. They'll believe anything they see in print.” *Charlotte's Web*
37. “This work was strictly voluntary, but any animal who absented himself from it would have his rations reduced by half.” *Animal Farm*
38. “And I like large parties. They're so intimate. At small parties there isn't any privacy.” *The Great Gatsby*
39. “Me and you, we got more yesterday than anybody. We need some kind of tomorrow.” *Beloved*
40. “They said they would rather be outlaws a year in Sherwood Forest than President of the United States forever.” *Tom Sawyer*
41. “The only thing worse than a boy who hates you: a boy that loves you.” *The Book Thief*
42. “It was written I should be loyal to the nightmare of my choice.” *Heart of Darkness*
43. “If you were to be lost in the river, Jonas, your memories would not be lost with you. Memories are forever.” *The Giver*
44. “If everybody minded their own business, the world would go around a great deal faster than it does.” *Alice in Wonderland*
45. “All human wisdom is contained in these two words - Wait and Hope.” *The Count of Monte Cristo*

Character Traits

Can you name the TV show based on three characters?

1. Abby Whelan, Cyrus Beene and Quin Perkins? *Scandal*
2. Timmy Patel, Jennifer Morgan and Russell Dunbar? *Rules of Engagement*
3. Jorah Mormont, Samwell, Tarly and Missandei? *Game of Thrones*
4. Tasha Yar, Guinan and Ro Laren? *Star Trek: The Next Generation*
5. Rob Petrie, Buddy Sorrell and Sally Rogers? *The Dick Van Dyke Show*
6. Gloria Mendoza, Joe Caputo and Piper Chapman? *Orange is the New Black*
7. Mike Biggs, Carl McMillan and Victoria Flynn? *Mike and Molly*
8. Toby Damon, Kate Pearson and William Hill? *This Is Us*
9. Raj Thomas, Mama Thomas and Dwayne Nelson? *What's Happening!!*
10. Jim Hopper, Joyce Byers and Eleven? *Stranger Things*
11. Cheryl Tunt, Pam Poovey and Ray Gillette? *Archer*
12. Frank Reynolds, Charlie Kelly and Mac? *It's Always Sunny in Philadelphia*
13. Cookie Lyon, Tiana Brown and Anika Calhoun? *Empire*
14. Charlene Frazier, Suzanne Sugarbaker and Mary Jo Shively? *Designing Women*
15. Alan Shore, Denise Bauer and Denny Crane? *Boston Legal*
16. Donald Mallard, Ziva David and Abby Sciuto? *NCIS: Naval Criminal Investigative Service*

17. Danny Reagan, Frank Reagan and Maria Baez? *Blue Bloods*
18. Vince Romano, Stacy Sheridan and Jim Corrigan? *T.J. Hooker*
19. Andy Dwyer, Ann Perkins and Ron Swanson? *Parks and Recreation*
20. Robert Crawley, Anna Bates and Thomas Barrow? *Downtown Abbey*
21. Seth Bullock, Alma Garrett and Dan Dority? *Deadwood*
22. Fiona Gallagher, Kevin Ball and Veronica Fisher? *Shameless*
23. Mr. Belding, Lisa Powers and Jessie Spano? *Saved by the Bell*
24. Teddy Flood, Maeve Millay and Dolores Abernathy? *Westworld*
25. Jess Day, Nick Miller and Winston Bishop? *New Girl*
26. Gina Waters-Payne, Pamela James and Tommy Strawn? *Martin*
27. Andy Sipowicz, Arthur Fancy and Diane Russell? *NYPD Blue*
28. Bender, Philip J. Fry and Turanga Leela? *Futurama*
29. Jack Shephard, Kate Austen and Sawyer Ford? *Lost*
30. J.D. Dorian, Perry Cox and Elliot Reid? *Scrubs*

What Movie Is That Line From?

"You Want a Piece of Me?!"

1. "A man confronts you, he is enemy. An enemy deserves no mercy." *The Karate Kid*
2. "I feel the need. The need for speed." *Top Gun*
3. "After all, tomorrow is another day!" *Gone with the Wind*
4. "Why, you stuck-up, half-witted, scruffy-looking nerf herder!" *The Empire Strikes Back*
5. "Greed, for lack of a better word, is good." *Wall Street*
6. "Look, spaghetti arms. This is my dance space. This is your dance space. I don't go into yours, you don't go into mine." *Dirty Dancing*
7. "Symmetrical book stacking. Just like the Philadelphia mass turbulence of 1947!" *Ghostbusters*
8. "You never really understand a person until you consider things from his point of view, until you climb inside of his skin and walk around in it." *To Kill a Mockingbird*
9. "I feel like I've been in a coma for the past twenty years. And I'm just now waking up." *American Beauty*
10. "In every class, there's always one joker who thinks that he's smarter than me. In this class, that happens to be you. Isn't it, Mayonnaise?" *An Officer and a Gentleman*
11. "Mr. Treehorn tells us that he had to eject you from his garden party; that you were drunk and abusive." *The Big Lebowski*
12. "I'm going to hit you so hard that when you wake up, your clothes will be out of style!" *The Goonies*
13. "Never rat on your friends, and always keep your mouth shut." *Goodfellas*

14. "I know everything there is to know about the greatest game ever invented." *Hoosiers*
15. "I am warning you, if you touch my drums, I will stab you in the neck with a knife." *Step Brothers*
16. "Learn it. Know it. Live it." *Fast Times at Ridgemont High*
17. "I have discovered you have to work twice as hard if it's honest." *Gone in 60 Seconds*
18. "Harry, the clock on that nine-foot nuclear weapon is ticking." *Armageddon*
19. "What we're dealing with here is a complete lack of respect for the law." *Smokey and the Bandit*
20. "In every job that must be done, there is an element of fun." *Mary Poppins*
21. "If I had one day when I didn't have to be all confused and I didn't have to feel that I was ashamed of everything. If I felt that I belonged someplace." *Rebel Without a Cause*
22. "Even though some of you are pretty thin, you all have fat hearts, and that's what matters." *Pitch Perfect*
23. "You my friend are responsible for delaying my rendezvous with star command!" *Toy Story*
24. "Money won is twice as sweet as money earned." *The Color of Money*
25. "What do you mean there's no ice? You mean I gotta drink this coffee hot?" *Clerks*
26. "I wrote you 365 letters. I wrote you every day for a year." *The Notebook*
27. "You're so money, and you don't even know it." *Swingers*
28. "I don't like violence, Tom. I'm a businessman. Blood is a big expense." *The Godfather*
29. "You take the van, I'll keep the dog." *Slapshot*
30. "I know this is a silly question before I ask it, but can you Americans speak any other language besides English?" *Inglorious Basterds*

31. "You played dodgeball? I loved dodgeball! Of course, I was the ball." *Monsters, Inc.*
32. "Madness, as you know, is like gravity. All it takes is a little push." *The Dark Knight*
33. "You know, like nunchuck skills, bow hunting skills, computer hacking skills. Girls only like guys who have great skills." *Napoleon Dynamite*
34. "All I ever wanted was a single thing worth fighting for." *Avatar*
35. "Going to Harvard is the only way I'm going to get the love of my life back." *Legally Blonde*
36. "Oh, yes. The woman in the picture is me." *Titanic*
37. "Look, why don't we play a game I know? Whoever is quietest for the longest time wins." *Up*
38. "I want the fairytale." *Pretty Woman*
39. "You can't wear black. It looks like you're going to a funeral." *Walk the Line*
40. You think I like avoiding my wife and kids to hang out with nineteen-year-old girls every day? *Old School*
41. "It's a trend in diamonds. Champagne. It's a nice stone." *Beautiful Girls*
42. "I do what I do best: I take scores. You do what you do best: Try to stop guys like me." *Heat*
43. "Can I sleep in your room? I don't wanna sleep on a hide-a-bed with Fuller. If he has something to drink, he'll wet the bed." *Home Alone*
44. "My father was fond of saying you need three things in life - a good doctor, a forgiving priest, and a clever accountant. The first two, I've never had much use for." *Schindler's List*
45. "What we've got here is failure to communicate." *Cool Hand Luke*
46. "I'm sorry I ruined your lives and crammed 11 cookies into the VCR." *Elf*

47. "Everybody stay exactly where you are! The party's over. Somebody stepped on the cake!" *The Guns of Navarone*
48. "I'll dance with you, but it's not like you're my dream girl or nothin'." *Saturday Night Fever*
49. "You billowing bale of bovine fodder!" *The Wizard of Oz*
50. "Every man dies. Not every man really lives." *Braveheart*

Thank You for Reading

I sincerely hope you enjoyed the book and learned some new trivia that you didn't already know, or remembered something you thought you'd forgotten. Trivia is fun and a passion of mine. Thank you for sharing it with me. Evan

Made in the USA
Middletown, DE
30 November 2018